The
Long-Distance
Relationship
Guide

Library of Congress Cataloging in Publication Number: 2004107263

ISBN: 978-1-59474-206-4

Printed in Singapore

Typeset in Rotis Sans Serif and Rotis Serif

Designed by Andrea Stephany
Illustrations by Rachell Sumpter

Distributed in North America by Chronicle Books
85 Second Street
San Francisco, CA 94105

10 9 8 7 6 5 4 3 2 1

Quirk Books
215 Church Street
Philadelphia, PA 19106
www.quirkbooks.com

The
Long-Distance
Relationship
Guide

Advice for the
Geographically Challenged

By Caroline Tiger

QUIRK BOOKS

PHILADELPHIA

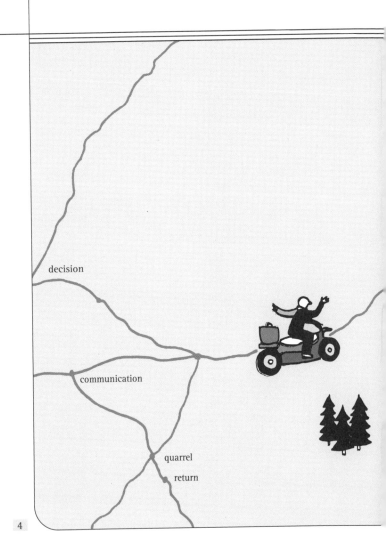

decision

communication

quarrel

return

Contents

run

true love

ldr pass

crossroads

rocky roads

drifter

If I had to say there was a survival kit for surviving a separation it would include: A good long-distance calling plan, a strong faith (whether it be God or just the sense that there are stronger forces in the universe than mere mortals), friends, books, Ben & Jerry's, a punching bag hanging in the garage, and a big box of wine in the fridge.

—Heidi, North Carolina

Having a long-distance relationship (LDR) is about as intuitive as walking up a down escalator . . . backward. It's like trying to find your glasses when you're not wearing your contact lenses. What's that you say? It's different for you? He or she is The One and a little thing like distance isn't going to keep you apart?

Well, okay, let me guess: You're a romantic type who cries every time you watch *Sleepless in Seattle*. Or maybe it's the opposite: You're an incredibly independent person who wants to be in a relationship but doesn't want your significant other so close that you'll actually have to see him every day. Either way, it's hard enough to have a relationship when you're in the same town—you've just made it much more difficult by deciding to go the long-distance route.

I know there are many more reasons for getting into an LDR, and for whatever reason you want your LDR to work, I agree that it's worth a shot. I only started out with the naysaying to break you down before I build you back up—it's called tough love. I did this for your own good, because in order to succeed in an LDR, you're going to need to toughen up.

You'll also need a sense of humor; a lot of hobbies to keep you busy during the time between phone calls and visits (having a career doesn't hurt); and a compact, sturdy travel bag. If you find it difficult to talk about your feelings over the phone or if you don't give good e-mail, you need to start developing these skills now. And if you're looking for assistance from any of the relationship books out there, you can stop looking—because LDRs come with a different set of problems from the ones that spring up in everyday close-range relationships.

So what makes me an expert? Since I don't claim to be, I did consult actual credentialed relationship experts. But I also drew from my own LDRs. (I'm beginning to worry that I'm turning into the serial long-distance dater I will warn you about in Chapter 2.) I knew it was a phenomenon when I got into my first LDR and it suddenly seemed as if everyone around me was in one, too, or had been in one at some point in their lives. At the magazine where I was on staff at the time, two of my coworkers were also boarding the commuter train from Philadelphia to New York City to see their LDPs (long-distance partners) every other weekend. We dubbed it the Love Train.

So why do so many of us put ourselves through the angst? I've given this a lot of thought, especially since I've been in three long-distance relationships, the third of which recently became short-distance. Two types of LDPs will generally answer this question in one of two ways:

THE ROMANTIC: *I've fallen head-over-heels for a person who fulfills all my romantic notions, and I'll be darned if I'm going to lose him/her over something as minor as distance.*

Once, on the train from Philadelphia to New York, I over-heard a man in his late 20s talking to a married, middle-aged woman. The seatmates had met just a few minutes before. The man was en route from Baltimore to Scranton, Pennsylvania, to see his girlfriend. They had become acquainted on-line a year before, and the first time he saw her in person, he thought to himself, "This is it. This feels right. I'm home." During these long train rides, he told his seatmate, "Whenever I begin to doubt myself, I just keep coming back to the same thought—that I can't imagine going through a day without talking to her."

THE PRAGMATIST: *I've seen enough of the local dating scene to know that I need to widen the net if I'm ever going to find a compatible partner.*

Once you've exhausted (read: dated and rejected) all of the geographically desirable options, you've no choice but to check out other area codes. The alternative—giving up, growing old alone, dying, and leaving all of your money to the pretty waitress at the corner diner—is just not a compelling plan for the future.

Whether you're a romantic or merely pragmatic, the following pages are your one-stop source for empathetic words, creative solutions, and expert advice from people who, like you, have decided to "go the distance." Included are real-life couples' accounts—both successes and horror stories—from people who've lived through what you're living through now. (Some of their names have been changed.) Their stories span miles of highway and sometimes even oceans and continents. They draw on the experiences and wisdom of long-haul truckers' wives, military couples, and serial LDPs from coast to coast.

Since this book first came out, I've realized that it's been missing one vital section, namely: What's next? What happens after one person moves and you're both in the same town? It's not just happily-ever-after and riding into the sunset and all that hooey. Believe me, I know. My boyfriend lives around the corner now. He moved here a few months ago. Now everything's ironed out, but in the beginning it wasn't so easy. The epilogue contains my and others' tips for this transition. The new section also has some other odds and ends, including readers' most frequent questions and a hall of fame of romantic gestures, also contributed by readers.

Remember to use these stories and friendly words of advice to enhance your own relationship, but try not to fall into the trap of *comparing* yourself to these couples. Every LDR is functional or dysfunctional in its own way. It's up to you to make the best of your own long-distance adventure.

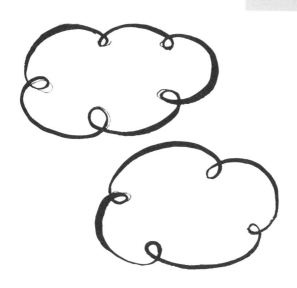

LDR Basics

As AN LDP AT THE BEGINNING OF THE TWENTY-FIRST CENTURY, you're both upholding an age-old institution and joining a tribe whose numbers continue to grow. But don't fool yourself into thinking that the modern trappings of e-mail, phones, planes, trains, and webcams will make your LDR easy. You need to be a certain kind of person—one with a peculiar combination of delusional tendencies, stick-to-it-iveness, romantic idealism, and communication skills.

You Are Not Alone: The LDR Stats

According to the most recent U.S. Census Bureau figures, about 2.4 million marriages are "commuter marriages," wherein one spouse moves to follow a job opportunity. This phenomenon crops up most often in weak economies, when job options are scarce. But for others, long-distance relationships are always a given. Couples in the military, academics, airline pilots, flight attendants, truckers, professional athletes, movie stars, and college students all contend with relocation (and dislocation) as a matter of course.

Gen Xers are the most likely to move long distances in search of work, according to 2000 Current Population Survey data. Add to this the 40 million Americans who have jobs that involve travel, resulting in more than 200 million business trips a year, and you have even more millions of LDPs. Ask around. You'll find that you're far from alone.

Why Stay Together?

That's the $64,000 question. Many of the couples I interviewed hardly thought about breaking up when one of them had to move away. Says Wendy, who left her boyfriend of a year in Vancouver when she moved to England, "There was no sense in breaking up just because people said it wouldn't work." She and her LDP figured that if they were making it work in the same town, they may as well give it a shot long distance.

Relationship experts advise that being in love is not enough to keep a pair together. To gauge whether this person is really The One, think about your compatibility in terms of your dreams for the future. Do you want the same lifestyle and number of kids? Do you want to live in a city or in the suburbs? Do you share a basic value system and consider your partner to be your best friend? If so, you may want to stick it out.

If you decide not to stick it out, and you break up before your partner moves away, be aware that the distance may end up bringing you back together. That's what happened to Neil and Makaylia, who broke up when Makaylia left New

York City to attend a law school outside of Philadelphia. The couple talked infrequently after her move, and Neil took the opportunity of being newly single to be extra social. "I was going to parties and meeting people—but I missed her," he remembers. "When I was out, I wanted her there with me, sharing it with me." Neil came to Philadelphia a few months after Makaylia's move to attend a Bassett hound festival, and he invited her to come along. They had a great day. "We sat in the grass," he recalls. "We had a picnic." Soon after, he called Makaylia and asked if she'd be interested in getting back together. She decided to give him another chance, and they dated long distance for a year until Neil moved to Philadelphia.

"Being apart drew us closer together. My going away made us talk about how serious we were sooner." —Mindy

Are You Cut Out for a Long-Distance Relationship?

What effect does absence have on you? Many relationship experts will tell you it does *not* make the heart grow fonder, that only closeness and the sharing of experiences can do that. But other experts postulate that yes, absence *can* make the heart grow fonder. And from these unscientific survey results, we can conclude the following definitive answer: It all depends.

If you're an optimistic person, one who sees a glass that is filled halfway as half-full, you may be more inclined to let absence work wonders on your heart and on your relationship. But if you see that glass as half-empty, you're more likely to despair and wallow during your time apart. Of course, it would be oversimplifying a very complicated situation to suggest that the success of an LDR depends entirely on the partners' attitudes. It doesn't. There are many other factors that can affect the fondness gauge, for better or worse.

Use the checklists on the following pages to help you determine your readiness to enter into an LDR.

☐ | Any of the following songs brings you to tears: "The Rose," "Crazy," "Unchained Melody."

☐ | Your favorite movie director is Nora Ephron.

☐ | You have no qualms talking on your cell phone in public.

☐ | You're a prolific e-mailer and/or own reams of writing paper and a calligraphy pen.

☐ | You like going to and learning about new places.

☐ | You've never cheated on a significant other.

☐ | You have no dependents.

☐ | You believe that there's one true love for everyone.

☐ | You're a phone sex god(dess).

☐ | You're independent and adventurous.

☐ Your favorite expression is "Romance, schmomance."

☐ Your favorite movie director is Wes Craven.

☐ You live in an area with horrible cell-phone reception.

☐ You can't write an entertaining and informative e-mail to save your life.

☐ You hate to travel.

☐ You have a hard time remaining faithful.

☐ Your pets, plants, and/or children suffer from intense separation anxiety.

☐ You think there are many people you could fall in love with: who you end up with is just a matter of timing.

☐ Getting on the phone and asking, "What are you wearing?" makes you erupt in a fit of giggles.

☐ You're a shut-in.

An Extremely Abridged History of LDRs

Should we stay together? How are we going to make it work? These age-old questions date back to prehistoric times. In early LDRs, it was almost exclusively the man who left home to hunt big game and fight wars. The women stayed behind. (It's possible that Viking wives were happy to see their men go, considering that Vikings were notorious for bad table manners and poor hygiene. But one can't assume such things.)

30,000 to 230,000 years ago: Neanderthal men leave early in the morning for hunting expeditions and do not return until late afternoon—a long time for men and women who are short on time. (Their average lifespan was 30 years.)

500 to 20 B.C.: Thousands of miles of roads are built for ancient Roman troops to patrol the huge empire they conquered. Little is recorded about the women they left behind.

A.D. 793 to 900: Viking raids on British Isles and northern France. Wives and steady girlfriends are left behind.

1577–1580: Sir Francis Drake circumnavigates the globe, leaving Mary Newman, his wife of eight years, back in England. His "business trip" lasts three years.

1750–1914 (Industrial Revolution): Huge advances in transport and travel. Roads are maintained; new bridges are built. In Britain, bicycles are in general use. In the later period, buses are introduced, and the first cars are built in Germany in 1885. These new modes of transportation lay the groundwork for future LDPs to travel to one another's homes.

1763–1783 (American Revolution): Colonial American wives take over farms and businesses while their husbands leave to fight the American Revolutionary War. These LDPs do not have the convenience of telephones or even reliable mail service to keep in contact.

1804: First steam locomotive built in England. Twenty years later, the first passenger railway opens, introducing the world to yet another means of travel that will prove useful for future LDPs' weekend visits.

1903: The Wright brothers make the first powered flight, paving the way for millions of future long-distance partners to fly to their loved ones.

1914–1919 and 1940–1945: Millions of men leave home to fight the World Wars raging overseas. Far-flung lovers and spouses communicate via snail mail that is monitored by army officers who censor secret information and look for signs of weakening morale.

1980s–1990s: Growing trend in commuter marriages in the U.S. as recession hits and people are forced to expand their job searches beyond their hometowns.

September 1991: *Griffin and Sabine*, by Nick Bantok, spends more than 50 weeks on the *New York Times* bestseller list. It's the story of a long-distance affair documented through postcards.

2000–2001: Hillary Clinton starts her first term as a New York senator, and Bill sets up office in Harlem. The duo seems to thrive on a schedule that finds them frequently apart.

February 2001: Hollywood couple Nicole Kidman and Tom Cruise announce their divorce, blaming their estrangement on the constant separation imposed by their hectic schedules—and giving LDRs a large dose of bad publicity.

December 2006: Distance is said to be the cause of yet another Hollywood break-up—this time between Jennifer Aniston and Vince Vaughn.

These couples' tales are the stuff of drama and tragedy. For them, the problem of distance was often compounded by more serious obstacles, including man-eating giants and overprotective fathers.

Penelope and Odysseus

In *The Odyssey*, the epic penned by Homer in the seventh century B.C., Odysseus is a victorious Greek hero who takes more than ten years to return home to his native Ithaka after fighting in the Trojan War. While his wife, Penelope, waits for his return, she bravely staves off bands of rowdy suitors. Meanwhile, Odysseus tries to make his way home but comes up against an angry sea god, an island full of tempting sirens, and another island populated with giant man-eating creatures. Finally Odysseus returns home and reunites with his loving and ever-faithful wife. (Inexplicably, Odysseus is allowed to have many affairs during his years at sea, but Penelope must remain faithful to him.)

Napoleon and Josephine

In March 1796, Napoleon and Josephine are married. Days after the wedding, Napoleon leaves to command the French army near Italy. Throughout the following months, he begs

Josephine to join him, and the couple exchange heated love letters. But soon after Josephine moves to Milan to be nearer to him, Napoleon begins to hear rumors of her infidelity. At one point he goes to her apartment in Milan and finds it empty. He waits for her for nine days. In March 1798, the general confronts his wife; she denies everything. Napoleon takes a lover in retaliation, and their relationship is never the same again. In 1809, Napoleon divorces Josephine after having a son with a mistress (proving that it is Josephine's, not Napoleon's, fault that the couple has not produced any children). Napoleon leaves Josephine to marry a woman who can bear him a legitimate heir.

Admiral Horatio Nelson and Emma Hamilton

Horatio meets Emma when he shows up in Naples, Italy, in 1798, having fought several nasty battles at sea. Emma is already married, to the British ambassador in Naples, Sir William Hamilton, but when Horatio arrives all bloody, beat-up, and dashingly dangerous, she takes it upon herself to nurse him back to health. When he is well enough, she accompanies him to social functions, where she acts as his translator. (She speaks seven languages.) It's unclear whether her husband is wise to the couple. Even after the Hamiltons move back to England and Emma bears a daughter named Horatia, the Hamiltons remain married. There are extended periods of separation throughout Nelson and Hamilton's seven-year affair, during which the admiral is away at sea, fighting more battles in the name of his queen. Their affair is documented in his many earthy love letters. A sample of his fiery prose: "What must be my sensations at the idea of sleeping with you! It sets me on fire, even the thoughts, much more would be the reality . . . Would to God I had dined with you tonight. What a dessert we would have had." The affair ends when the admiral is killed in battle in 1805.

Elizabeth Barrett and Robert Browning

Robert reads Elizabeth's poem, "Lady Geraldine's Courtship," in 1844, and immediately wants to meet the woman who has written the verses that stir his heart. But Elizabeth is an invalid and a recluse who is kept shut in by her tyrannical father; he forbids any of his adult children to marry. A family friend arranges a meeting, explaining to Elizabeth's father that Robert is a fan of his daughter's poetry. Soon afterward, Robert professes his love for Elizabeth in a letter that begins, "I love your verses with all my heart, dear Miss Barrett."

The two exchange 574 letters during their 20-month courtship. Since Elizabeth's father is so protective, the lovers hardly ever see each other in the flesh—that is, until they wed secretly in 1846 and run away to Italy. Elizabeth is 40 years old and Robert is 34.

Mia Farrow and Woody Allen

The famous director and his muse live in separate apartments on either side of Central Park in New York City for part of the 12 years they are together. Woody lives on the west side of the park, and Mia on the east side. According to Mia's 1997 memoir, *What Falls Away*, part of the reason they live apart is because Allen has zero interest in kids, and Mia has three biological children and three adopted kids from her marriage to Andre Previn. As Mia continues to accumulate children, Woody and Mia visit each other almost every day until Woody is found having an affair with one of Mia's adopted children, and the relationship dissolves.

Two Major Types of LDRs

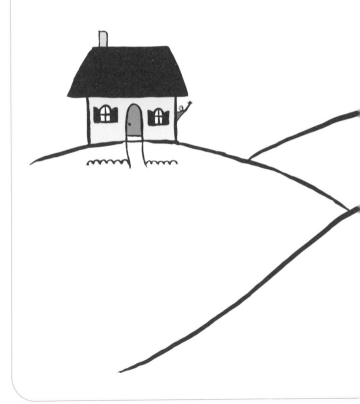

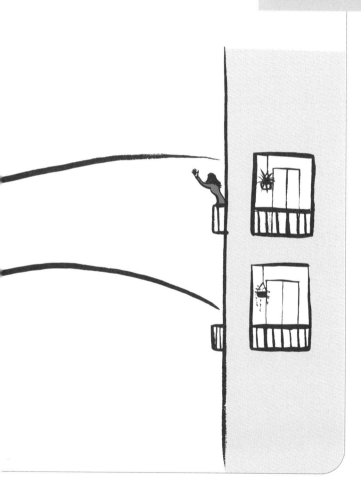

Now THAT LDRS HAVE BEEN PUT INTO HISTORICAL CONTEXT, you may be wondering what kind of LDR you've gotten yourself into. Chances are yours will not be as tragic as the LDRs outlined in Chapter 1. Hopefully yours is more akin to the Brownings', with their passionate love letters, than to Mia and Woody's, with their neuroses and question-able parent-child relations. Whatever the degree of drama, it should fit into one of two strains of modern LDRs: those that *turn* long distance (TLDRs) and those that *start* long distance (SLDRs).

Relationships That Turn Long Distance (TLDRs) and Commuter Marriages

DEFINITION: You've been dating or married for a while, and one of you has had to relocate indefinitely for school, work, career, military duties, family (to care for an aging parent; to be closer to kids from a previous marriage), or for a finite amount of time, such as summer camp or a semester abroad.

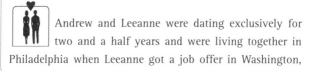 Andrew and Leeanne were dating exclusively for two and a half years and were living together in Philadelphia when Leeanne got a job offer in Washington,

D.C., that she couldn't turn down. "It was one of the things I hadn't yet crossed off on my list of what I want to do in life," says Leeanne. After she moved to D.C., the couple saw each other nearly every weekend during their two years living apart. They planned their wedding during this time and married while they were still living in different cities. Leeanne eventually moved back to Philadelphia.

≡ COUPLE CASE STUDY ≡

Andrew, 36, pharmaceutical market research, and Leeanne, 34, radio executive

Dependents: 0

Pets: 1 (Molly the cat)

Distance: Philadelphia, PA, to Washington, D.C. = 145 miles

L-D for: Two years

Frequency of visits: Varied from once a week to once a month

Their advice: Keep up on each other's day-to-day happenings through constant communication and by whatever means possible—have five-minute cell phone conversations through the course of the day, e-mail and text message each other, and invest in videophones and digital cameras.

Status at press time: Married and living in the same place

TLDR Pros and Cons

Though some experts think that TLDRs have a better chance at survival than SLDRs because they have a foundation to fall back on when the going gets tough, these couples also have more to lose. Throughout this section, and throughout the course of this book, we'll draw on the advice of two groups of seasoned TLDR pros: military spouses, who weather months and even years apart, and truckers' wives, who have lots of down-to-earth advice to offer LDPs, from coping techniques to how to make the most of the time spent together.

PROS

Time spent together is more meaningful. Whether you see each other every weekend or one weekend a month, those 32 to 48 hours (depending on your commute) will become precious. You may even revert back to honeymoon-stage behavior, when you want to spend every available moment with your partner.

> "You have to commit to being intimate with the person whenever you are together, because it's not just second nature like it is when you're together all the time."
> —Andrew

You have more individual freedom when apart. You don't have to check with your partner before making weekday or weeknight plans. You're more free to make plans with friends and have time to yourself.

"Develop a two-sided personality: the 'single' side, who eats out a lot and does exactly what she wants when she wants to do it, and the 'married' side, or the person you become when your husband comes home, when you cook and clean and do all those other wifely chores he expects."
—Lynne, trucker's wife for 13 years

You have more opportunities for adventure and the promise of new experiences. New restaurants, friends, walks, shops, take-out pizza places—visiting and living in a new place shakes off the shroud of predictability that may have settled on your relationship.

You may have more opportunities to learn new skills and take on responsibilities you never thought you could do. Maybe you're a newly minted Mr. Mom who's never had to see to the cooking, cleaning, and carpooling. Maybe you're accustomed to your spouse doing all the gardening and fix-it jobs around the house. Whatever the case, this might be a golden opportunity to tap into capabilities you never knew you had.

CONS

Lack of everyday talk. You're not able to meet up every night to exchange the minutiae of your day, from kvetching over the traffic you encountered on the way to work to commiserating about your annoying coworker's bad hygiene habits. These, after all, are the kinds of details on which intimacy is built.

Lack of everyday touch. More critically, you don't have the luxury of snuggling with your partner on the couch for an evening of trashy TV. Physical cues can provide a sense of security and togetherness that's hard to establish over the phone. (On the need for constant communication between LDPs, see Chapter 4.)

"Have him call you every night so you know he's alive."—*Debbie, trucker's wife for 1½ years*

The loss of "couple" friends. Let's face it: Couples like to socialize with other couples. Maybe they feel uncomfortable when there's a single person present; they feel guilty holding hands and kissing each other in front of someone who's not about to be on the receiving end of that tender loving care anytime soon. When your LDP finally does come to town, group get-togethers may feel forced or awkward because the four of you have not had the opportunity for spontaneous socializing.

Missing major milestones and events. This may include a child's first steps, a spouse's birthday, or even caring for an ill pet.

Hardship Perks for the Working TLDR

Are you being transferred to Toledo? When life hands you lemons, make lemonade.

You may have rationalized your way through some of the above-mentioned pros and cons, but at the end of the day, long distance really *isn't* the next best thing to being there. If travel and relocation are not part of the job you signed on for (e.g., you are not in the military or the air travel industry), you might want to consider having a heart-to-heart talk with your employer. Point out the hardship of the situation and politely suggest some ways that will help you and your LDP contend with the move. Here are some benefits to ask for:

Living and traveling expenses. Have the company put money toward your living expenses in the new city as well as toward your travel expenses, since you and your spouse will be flying, driving, and training to and fro as much as possible.

Flexible hours. Consider asking your boss for a flexible schedule that will allow you a full block of days with your family. This doesn't necessarily mean working fewer hours—maybe you'll work four longer days in exchange for a Friday or Monday off to spend a three-day weekend with your LDP or family.

Telecommuting. See if you can do some of your job from your family's or partner's home. Even one week a month or one day a week can make a difference.

Bonus. Consider asking for a bonus to compensate for the extra expenses that go into maintaining two homes. (No matter how inexpensive you make the second home, you'll still have to buy all of the basics—cleaning supplies, bedding, curtains, etc.—along with your food and traveling expenses.) Ask that the bonus be based on your performance or your department's performance (if you're a manager) and agree on scheduling a performance review within three or six months to assess how well the arrangement is working out.

Advice from Lifers: Military Spouses

Marrying into the military means marrying into a potentially indefinite long-distance relationship. The certainty of this doesn't ease the situation much, but military families do benefit from the tight-knit community left behind when the troops are deployed. That built-in support network leaves military LDPs better equipped than mere civilians to handle the long absences, although deployments present another set of anxieties and uncertainties. The following survival tips come from military spouses who are eager to share their hard-won wisdom. (Unfortunately, no military husbands contributed, but we know they're out there!)

TIP #1: HAVE A SENSE OF HUMOR

"We laugh about all the mini catastrophes that only seem to happen while Daddy is gone. Believe a military wife when she tells you that:

- her kids are never ill when hubby is home
- her appliances never break down when he is around
- toilets do not clog or overflow
- children do not break bones
- there are no hurricanes, tornadoes, or floods

It's not Murphy's Law, it's Military Law."

—Heidi, North Carolina

TIP #2: KEEP YOUR SPOUSE FRESH IN YOUR CHILDREN'S MINDS

"It is our family ritual to both lay our son down and tell him good night. So hubby makes sure he calls right as I am laying him down. I pass the phone to my son, and my hubby chats with him a bit and tells him good night. Then I have the rest of the night to talk without interruptions."

—Marci, Maryland

"My kids have a 'Daddy Board.' It's simply a bulletin board in their room. Every photograph, letter, and postcard from Dad is a coveted item and is pinned onto this board in

addition to the last photos we took before he deployed."
—Heidi, North Carolina

"When my husband was deployed, our son was only five months old. So he missed his son's first word, the first time he crawled, his first steps, when he started eating more solid food. Of course I never had the camcorder going when our son did those things for the first time, but I got the second or third times on video."
—Kristen, California

"Our screensaver on the computer is pictures of Dad. It's hard for my hubby to send my son presents other than homemade ones right now, so I wrap up special things and mail them to my son from Dad."
—Marci, Maryland

TIP #3: HAVE A REALLY ROMANTIC AND RESOURCEFUL LDP
(Note: This is one of those pages you should earmark when you leave this book out for your LDP to see.)

"My husband was preparing to get deployed and it was going to be the first time he was gone over Christmas. I was very upset, but I went on about my life. I got a letter in the mail two days before Christmas, and it was a treasure map of my own home. It led me to my Christmas presents that he bought and hid four months prior. I didn't even suspect it the whole time."

—Marci, Maryland

Relationships That Start Long Distance (SLDRs)

DEFINITION: You met while on vacation, by long-distance setup, or online.

 Megan C. and Tim were set up on a blind date by their parents' friends, and they could tell at that first dinner that there was a spark. "There was something more," Megan remembers. "A connection." Though she lived in Boston and he lived in Albany, New York, they decided to give it a shot. Within two months, they had decided to date exclusively and did so long distance for a year and a half. Before they got married, the longest they had spent in each other's company was a week and a half.

Megan C., 26, attorney, and Tim, 28, attorney/marine reservist

Dependents/pets: 0

Distance: Boston, MA, to Albany, NY = 175 miles

L–D for: One and a half years

Frequency of visits: Every weekend

Their advice: Be up front from the beginning about your feelings and what you want out of the relationship. There's no room for game-playing in an LDR.

Status at press time: Married and living in the same city

The Long-Distance Courtship

Getting to know someone over e-mail and the telephone is a challenging exercise at best. Relationship counselor Margaret Shapiro suggests that if you meet a person on vacation, you hit it off, and he truly seems like someone you want to pursue, you should try to get to know him from all sides. Stay with him for more than two days at a time so you can see him when he's cranky and tired as well as when he's charming and "on." "Otherwise," she says, "it can be a kind of make-believe relationship where you're projecting onto him whatever you think he's like."

And even if you feel like you know how he would act day to day, because you're familiar with his general ideas and value system, oftentimes actions speak louder than words. Meet his family and friends, advises Shapiro: "Don't just live on your little island together." Whether it's casual or more, make sure you want the same out of the relationship and are both taking it equally as lightly or seriously.

Here are three ways to go about the long-distance courtship, based on one hypothetical couple.

A couple meets at a wedding in, say, Louisiana. He's from Austin, Texas. She's from Manhattan. They hit it off at the wedding, spend most of the weekend together, and end up exchanging phone numbers. Once back home, they have several great phone conversations.

GO FOR BROKE
(RISK LEVEL: HIGH)

They decide that he's going to come to New York and stay with her for five days. This is the Why Waste Time tactic, which is great for getting to the point as soon as possible. Try this method if you're thinking, "This person is The One." At the end of spending 24 hours a day together for five days, you'll be a lot better informed.

Another go-for-broke tactic is to meet halfway and take a three- or four-day road trip together. Nothing tests a relationship like hours trapped in a car.

THE COLLEGE TRY
(RISK LEVEL: MEDIUM)

After the great phone conversations, they decide that he'll come to New York, where he has some good friends, for a long weekend. The two will spend time together, but he'll be staying at his friend's apartment, so there's no pressure for them to hit it off and spend the night together. If that goes well, they plan another visit, either at a halfway point or on his home turf. If the second date goes well, they plan a third, which, if all signs are still pointing to go, results in the "Let's date exclusively" conversation.

(Note: It may seem premature to have this conversation after only three dates, but in LDR time, three dates is equivalent to at least six conventional dates. And considering the time and effort that go into seeing each other, it's best to proceed with an LDR *only* if you like the person enough to date him or her exclusively.)

"At the beginning we talked every two days. We got to know a lot about each other by talking on the phone."
—Megan C.

SLOW AND STEADY
(RISK LEVEL: LOW)
Instead of planning visits right away, the couple gets to know each other over more phone calls and e-mail. This is trickier, since they don't have the face-to-face falling-for-each-other time that is the glue of any LDR—these are the moments LDPs call to mind when they're really missing each other. There's something to be said for getting to know each

other slowly, but experts advise using all modes of communication at your disposal, including face-to-face interaction, so that you can better determine your compatibility. E-mail can be especially deceiving (see page 52 for an in-depth explanation).

Of course, once a slow-and-steady LDR becomes at all serious, it will need to shift into a higher gear.

"When you're in the same place, you might worry that you're spending too much time together, and since you want to take it slow, you pull away. That's not a concern when you're getting to know each other long distance."
—Megan A.

Pro or con? It all depends on your attitude.

Pros

- Honeymoon period typically lasts twice as long.

- Distance makes romantic courtship rituals (love letters, mixed tapes, surprise gifts and visits) more likely to occur.

- You're less likely to hang onto it if it's not working.

- It's a great alternative when you're fed up with the pool of geographically convenient candidates.

- You'll have sex sooner.

- Your partner has no way of gauging your behavior during the time between visits.

Cons

- Faults (bad hygiene, moodiness, infidelity) are revealed at a much slower pace.

- Increased number of romantic gestures will give you high expectations that can't possibly be met once you finally do live close-range.

- Because of the effort put into the relationship, you may decide to stick it out just to convince yourself that all of that time, money, and aggravation were worth it.

- You have less of a chance of meeting someone who's more geographically desirable.

- You'll have to deal with sex sooner.

- You'll have no way of gauging your partner's behavior during the time between visits.

E-mail and the SLDR

Technology can be deceiving. E-mail can foster a false sense of intimacy and make you feel like you know a person well when you really don't. You'll learn more about the vagaries of communication for LDRs in Chapter 4, but for the time being keep in mind that, when embarking on a long-distance relationship—especially one that starts out long distance—you should use e-mail communication to *supplement* telephone conversations, not vice versa. When face-to-face communication is not possible, the only way to truly get to know someone is through real-time conversation.

In the meantime, use the following personality indicators to help read between the lines of your potential LDP's e-mails.

E-MAIL RED FLAGS

- Excessive use of exclamation points: Sender may be insecure and ruled by a need to be liked by everyone.

- Stilted, formal e-mail style (may open with "Dear" and close with "Sincerely"): Sender may be uptight and averse to spontaneity; may also reveal that sender came of age before e-mail was widespread.

- Sentimental sig line: Sender likes Hallmark cards and will resort to traditionally romantic gestures, such as sending bouquets of red roses and arranging candlelit dinners.

- Evasive, doesn't answer questions: Sender may be concealing something—such as a husband or boyfriend or criminal record. Be cautious and trust your instincts.

- Eager to share war stories from past relationships: Sender may be a serial committer who jumps from relationship to relationship, indicating neediness and lack of independence.

- Whines, complains, obsesses about problems: Sender very easily assumes the mantle of victim or martyr and is just as likely to do so in an interpersonal relationship.

How to Avoid a Fatal Attraction

Glenn Close's character in *Fatal Attraction* has a borderline personality disorder—and by the time Michael Douglas suspects that something about her is a little off, the rabbit is, shall we say, cooked. Don't let this happen to you. It's easy for someone with borderline or narcissistic personality disorder to appear well-adjusted from a distance. That's why, says criminal psychologist Dr. John Dicke, these kinds of people are attracted to long-distance relationships. "They can talk the talk," he says. "But they don't have to walk the walk." Here are some danger signs to watch out for:

She falls in love way too fast. You're the one for her. She knows it. There's no use looking any further. She *loves* you, e-mails you ten times a day, calls every night—all within the first few weeks of meeting you. **Indicates:** Someone who has no boundaries and is excessively needy.

He drops names, net worth, luxe vacation spots. He lets you know right off the bat that he power lunches at a prominent steakhouse, that he has a Beamer, and that he pulls in major bills. **Indicates:** Someone with a weak sense of self who identifies with material objects and the superficially grandiose. When you get to know him, you'll probably find that he's been exaggerating, and that he's barely hanging on by his fingernails.

She treats waitstaff, pets, children, and others badly. She talks down to anyone perceived as less powerful. **Indicates:** Someone who will eventually treat you that way, too.

There are no family photos, pets, plants, or souvenirs in his apartment. He possesses no artifacts of human relatedness— no straw hat from the trip to Mexico with his buddies, no photo of him holding his baby god-daughter. **Indicates:** Intimacy issues—someone who may be comfortable having a relationship from afar but once you become close-range, will reveal excessive dysfunctions.

Someone who's willing to have a long-distance romance based on one meeting or even sight unseen (for example, after a series of e-mail exchanges), might be a **serial long-distance dater** who is either intentionally or subconsciously seeking a partner who will be in town only on weekends. Some warning signs of an unwillingness to commit include:

1. His face actually lights up when you tell him where you live (and it's far away).

2. He pays his phone bill using a frequent-flyer credit card.

3. He has huge collections of airline alcohol bottles, travel-sized toiletries, and weekend bags.

4. Her apartment's décor can only be described as "transitional": there is no art on the walls; the bed is a mattress on the floor; and she has no pets or plants.

5. She has had more than two long-term long-distance relationships.

6. She was the one who broke off her previous long-term long-distance relationships.

7. He talks a lot about maintaining his freedom and independence, even while he's in the long-distance relationship. He may even use the phrase "flexing my freedom muscle."

8. She laughs, sighs, and/or changes the subject when you talk about future plans that involve the two of you living in the same town.

9. He never introduces you to any of his friends and family.

10. When you joke about his "weekday girlfriend," there is a long pause before he laughs.

The serial long-distance dater has commitment issues that are separate from your relationship and cannot be resolved through yet *another* long-distance pairing. This relationship will probably end with you issuing an ultimatum—move or cut bait. Beware: Chances are that the serial dater will choose the latter.

An Indefinite LDR à la Mia and Woody

Despite the title of this chapter, there is one last, very rare type of LDR that does not fit into either of the major types discussed. We include it here to show that some LDRs defy easy categorization; long-distance partners may in fact blaze an entirely new path because they have found a way of life that works perfectly for them.

DEFINITION: You and your partner decide to live apart indefinitely. This is the rarest of situations—most LDPs have a long-term plan that involves living in the same town someday.

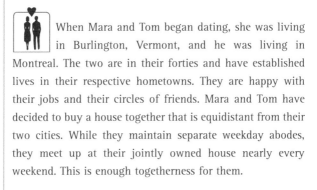 When Mara and Tom began dating, she was living in Burlington, Vermont, and he was living in Montreal. The two are in their forties and have established lives in their respective hometowns. They are happy with their jobs and their circles of friends. Mara and Tom have decided to buy a house together that is equidistant from their two cities. While they maintain separate weekday abodes, they meet up at their jointly owned house nearly every weekend. This is enough togetherness for them.

COUPLE CASE STUDY

Mara, 44, sales, and Tom, 47, banking

Dependents/pets: 0

Distance: Burlington, VT, to Montreal, Quebec = 97 miles

L-D for: Three years

Frequency of visits: Nearly every weekend

Their advice: Make your lives together in whatever way makes you happy. Don't hesitate to take the less conventional path along the way.

Status at press time: Together, apart

The Visit

THE VISIT—WHETHER IT LASTS FOR A WEEKEND OR A WEEK—is the centerpiece of every long-distance relationship. It's the reward at the end of every long period of separation, and for that reason, long-distance couples put a lot of pressure on the weekend's success. They want everything to be just right.

But no weekend is perfect. There are all kinds of things that can go wrong: The zit that announces its presence midweek inevitably becomes a full-blown menace on your forehead come Friday evening. A frustrating commute renders the person who's visiting in a foul mood, not to mention three hours late. The restaurant where you made reservations for Saturday night closes early due to a bizarre and unprecedented kitchen mishap.

There are many circumstances beyond your control, which is why it's important to focus on the fact that you're *together*. The best visits occur when you're prepared to handle some of the more inevitable glitches—the factors that *are* in your control.

Duration and Frequency

Duration and frequency of visits depend, of course, on the relationship and on the distance between you, but both partners should agree upon a mutually workable pattern of visits at the very outset.

Finding a Balance

All of the long-distance partners I interviewed for this book determined how often they'd see each other based on four key factors:

1. The physical distance between them. Are you long-distance (more than three hours' driving time apart) or middle-distance (between one and three hours)?

2. How much time apart they could withstand.

3. How many visits per month were logistically and financially feasible.

4. How many visits per month they could make without feeling like they were losing hometown friends and/or shirking hometown responsibilities (such as a regular volunteering gig or being there for kids, pets, and other family members).

 At one extreme are Kurtis and Wendy, who lived, respectively, in Vancouver, British Columbia, and Oxford, England, for one and a half years. Their visits were spaced as far apart as once every six months, but those visits lasted one to two weeks each. After receiving enormous phone bills the month after Wendy moved to England, they realized they could afford to speak on the phone only about once a week. Since the long-distance portion of their relationship occurred in the late 1980s, in the B.E. (Before E-mail) era, their communication was limited. Their relationship worked because both were and are extremely independent creatures and were unwavering in their belief that they were meant for each other.

COUPLE CASE STUDY

Wendy, 27, journalist, and Kurtis, 28, restaurant manager
Dependents/pets: 0
Distance: Oxford, England, to Vancouver, British Columbia
= 4500 miles
L–D for: One and a half years
Frequency of visits: One- to two-week visits every few months.
Their advice: Write intense and romantic letters (especially if the alternative is paying for international calls) and send lots of care packages. Make new friends and learn to enjoy your own company instead of spending the entire time thinking about and missing your LDP.
Status at press time: Married and living in Vancouver

At the other extreme are Cher and Elias, who lived, respectively, in Washington, D.C., and Charlottesville, Virginia. They agreed right away that they would talk on the phone every night and would see each other every weekend. Wendy and Kurtis are still together. Cher and Elias are not. This proves that there's no "right" way to do it. One way doesn't guarantee success more than any other. What matters most is that it feels right—and doable—for both of you.

=== COUPLE CASE STUDY ===

Cher, 29, PR agent, and Elias, 28, financial advisor
Dependents/pets: 0
Distance: Washington, D.C., to Charlottesville, Virginia = 115 miles
L-D for: One year and three months
Frequency of visits: Every weekend
Their advice: Make a serious commitment to each other, and talk often about that commitment.
Status at press time: Broken up

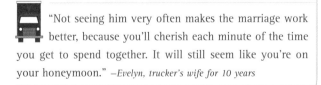 "Not seeing him very often makes the marriage work better, because you'll cherish each minute of the time you get to spend together. It will still seem like you're on your honeymoon." —*Evelyn, trucker's wife for 10 years*

As you begin to visit your LDP more regularly, your pet may begin to experience separation anxiety. Here are some telltale symptoms that they're suffering:

TYPE OF PET	TYPICAL NEUROTIC BEHAVIOR
DOG	Destructiveness; inappropriate urinating and defecating; excessive salivating; vocalization
CAT	Overattachment to owner; "protest urination" or defecation; sulking, crying, or hiding as you are getting ready to leave; cat anorexia (refusing food, especially while you're gone)
HAMSTER	Hair loss, skin warts due to compulsive grooming
BIRD	Overgrooming and feather-plucking

SOLUTIONS:

- Get another pet so your primary pet has a playmate, but don't leave the two alone for more than a day until they are accustomed to one another.

- Leave a light on and the radio playing low so the pet feels like she has company and isn't too traumatized by outside noises or, on the flip side, by silence. Leave your curtains open, so your pet has some changing scenery upon which to gaze.

- Ask a friend to drop by, not just to feed or walk your pet, but to hang out for a while in your house or apartment to give your pet some regular companionship.

- Ask your vet about anxiety medication.

Negotiating Turn-Taking

All things are not equal. One of you may have a car and the other does not. One of you may have a six-figure job, and the other earns, well, less than six figures. One of you may have a job that requires long-distance postings on a regular basis, and the other may work five minutes from home. Other factors to take into account besides money and means of transport include:

- flex time allowed by your job/school schedule
- dependents (kids/pets)
- capacity to telecommute
- desirability of location and quality/cleanliness of homes (her tiny apartment in Hicksville or his fully loaded duplex in the swinging urban neighborhood?)

All of these considerations come into play when you're deciding who's going to visit whom and how often, but no two couples are alike. As you'll see in the following scenarios, negotiation and compromise can take on many different forms.

Couple #1: She's a partner in a law firm, makes lots of money, and has a car. He's a freelance graphic designer who, because he recently changed careers, is just starting out and living paycheck to paycheck. He also has a car.

Who should visit whom more often? Since he has a more flexible schedule, he should visit her more often than she visits him. Chances are she's working longer, more demanding hours, whereas he can telecommute. She may offer to pay his auto expenses–gas and parking–to make up for the inconvenience. She should also surprise him every now and then with the gift of a book on tape that he'll enjoy while he's driving.

Couple #2: He's divorced with two kids he sees every Sunday. She has no kids, but her cat suffers from major separation anxiety every time she leaves home.

Who should visit whom more often? Sorry. Kids trump cats. She should look into finding a friend who will agree to sleep over at her place while she's out of town, or get another cat to keep the first one company–or board the cat at the vet so it doesn't destroy her apartment out of anxiety. Her LDP should try to arrange to spend some weekends at her home– no LDR should be so one-sided, unless both partners are in complete agreement. If the relationship has moved into a

more permanent stage, he may want to have his children visit as well.

Couple #3: He still lives with his parents. She has her own place.

Who should visit whom: Are you kidding? He should always, always visit her. And if he's older than 22, she should rethink the whole relationship.

Visit Preparedness Checklist
Whether you're the visiting or visited LDP, make sure the

following items are checked off and accounted for beforehand.

VISITOR

☐ Travel-sized toiletries

☐ Wrinkle-free clothing (synthetic fabrics,
cotton/lycra blends)

☐ Work to do or book to read in case you
run out of things to say (or experience
travel delays)

☐ Prescription meds

☐ Birth control

☐ Clothing/jewelry given to you by
your LDP

HOST

☐ Partner's favorite foods

☐ Partner's favorite booze

☐ Birth control

☐ Clean sheets and towels

☐ Prominently displayed
pictures of you and your LDP

☐ Clothing/jewelry given to you by
your LDP

You may have been so busy during the week that you didn't have time to tidy up. Here are some tips for speed-cleaning.

1. **Put on some entertainment.** Choose some dance music that you can sing along to or a book on tape to keep your mind occupied.

2. **Tackle the clutter.** Make the rounds of your place holding two bags: one for trash, the other for everything else. Pick a starting point and make your way around the place clockwise, not letting yourself get distracted at any point.

3. **Dust.** Using an electromagnetic dust cloth (like Swiffer), work your way around again clockwise, dusting every surface you come across from top to bottom.

4. **Vacuum.** Make sure you get into the corners and along the floorboards. Don't worry about going beneath and behind furniture—this is only a surface cleaning.

5. **Dispose of clutter.** Remember that bag of "everything else" from step 2? Unless there's something in it you'll need that

weekend, throw the whole thing in a closet, to be sorted and organized later.

6. **Bathroom/kitchen surface cleaning.** Again, focus on the superficial and obvious.

   - Clean the bathroom after a hot bath or shower; the steam will have loosened the dirt.

   - Definitely use a toilet cleaner.

   - Spritz and wipe off surfaces with lemony disinfectant.

   - Empty the sink of dishes.

7. **Disguise funky odors.** Light strong-smelling candles or incense. Dab perfume or cologne on a light bulb—the heat produced when the light is on will release the aroma.

8. **Dim lights for good measure.**

Arrivals: Great Expectations

As you wait for your partner's arrival, it's only natural to feel anxious. Those butterflies in your stomach are as fluttery as they are before a first date with someone you think is really cute. And it *is* kind of like a first date—chances are, you haven't seen your partner in a while. What if she's changed? What if there's something about him that's unfamiliar—a mannerism you've never seen, a strange new configuration of facial hair? Even though you've been talking or e-mailing every day, you will be unaccustomed to your partner's physical presence.

The Initial Awkwardness

There's a lot of pressure to start off the weekend like Kermit and Miss Piggy in *The Muppet Movie*, running toward each other in slow motion, arms spread, across a field of waving grain while a romantic ballad—preferably circa 1982—plays in the background. But here's the reality: You're about to spend an entire weekend with someone you haven't seen in at least a week, probably longer. You may even be filled with a vague sense of dread at seeing the person you've been idealizing suddenly take on human form.

"There were weekends when we felt we had to get reacquainted; the first few hours we were stiff. After a few weeks, I said, 'This isn't fun to waste four hours of our time being stiff and awkward,' so we talked about it and got past it."—Andrew

You may need to test out a few different scenarios to figure out what works best for you once your LDP arrives. Maybe you prefer to decompress after a couple of hours of traveling: Would you rather hang out on the couch for a while instead of being picked up at the airport and whisked off to a dinner with ten of your LDP's friends? Maybe you'd rather flip those activities so you're not immediately alone, face-to-face with your LDP, experiencing that period of initial awkwardness so soon.

Tips for Conquering the Jitters

Part of the challenge is being proactive about making your LDP feel comfortable with you and your home. Here are some ways to go about doing just that.

TIP #1: KEEP YOURSELF OCCUPIED BEFOREHAND.

Host: While you're waiting, put on some music and sing along while you alphabetize your books or CDs. Especially for visits that occur early in the relationship, assess the state of your towels, sheets, bathmats, and shower curtain. Are they soiled, frayed, threadbare, mildewy? If so, make a quick trip to the nearest housewares store for replacements. (See pages 72–73 for further cleaning instructions.)

Visitor: If you're a passive traveler (e.g., flying or taking a train instead of driving), bring work to do or a book to read to keep your mind off your impending reunion. If you are driving, invest in a book on tape or listen to talk radio.

TIP #2: CREATE A DIVERSION.

Host: Have your LDP meet you somewhere out on the town

or out with friends. If you know you need to run some errands, ask him to meet you at the hardware store or the supermarket. If your officemates go to happy hour after work on Friday, consider accompanying them and asking your LDP to meet you there. Conduct your initial meeting in a place where there's some outside stimuli to take the focus off the two of you.

Visitor: Arrive with a gift. Something funny and/or sweet will smooth the first few minutes and give you both a place to focus your attention and something to do with your hands. Bring your LDP a funny souvenir from your hometown, bake some brownies, or buy some fresh flowers on the way to his apartment.

Tip #3: MAKE BOTH HOMES COMFORTABLE.

Host: Stock the fridge with your LDP's favorite food and drinks. Clean out a drawer and carve out a space in your closet for her to store and hang her clothes.

Visitor: Leave some stuff at your partner's apartment—buy extra bottles of saline, shampoo, conditioner, moisturizing lotion, shaving cream, etc., and leave them there so you don't have to lug these items around each time you travel. If you go to the gym during every visit, leave a pair of sneakers. Buy an extra pair of slippers for your partner's place.

TIP #4: IF ALL ELSE FAILS, JUST START MAKING OUT.

That's right. Drop your bags and go at it—but agree beforehand that this is the plan of action. This can act as an icebreaker—it's funny and ridiculous. And it will give you something to talk about all weekend.

"When he *is* home, love him with all you got! He needs all the love you have so when he is out there all alone, he will be able to make it until the next time he pulls into home base. Have a smile waiting for him. Even if you don't feel like it all the time."—*Marilyn, trucker's wife for 11 years*

Activity Planning

For those SLDRs who are courting each other long-distance and deciding whether or not to pursue a relationship, couples counselor Margaret Shapiro suggests making good use of each visit as a sort of assessment tool. "Have longer visits and be sure that you pay attention to different sides of a visit," she advises. "Do something that's fun but also have time when you do some work. Can you spend quiet time together? Are you able to study or read a paper when you're together?" Are your activity levels well-matched, or would you rather stay home and rent a movie while he's itching to go clubbing? These are all measures of compatibility.

"When you're used to doing whatever you want all week, it's hard to integrate back into 'couples' mode,' when you're compromising over everything, from where to go to dinner to when to wake up."—Tim

The more answers you and your LDP have in common, the more activity compatible you are.

1. **On Friday night, at the end of a long week, I'm:**
   a. Ready and raring to go out on the town. Just give me 20 minutes for a power nap.
   b. Too exhausted to do anything but veg out on the couch.

2. **On Saturday night, I'd rather:**
   a. Go clubbing.
   b. Cook dinner together at home and rent a movie.

3. **On Sunday morning, I like to:**
   a. Wake up early and go for a jog.
   b. Sleep in, then go out for brunch.

4. **I think going to a museum is . . .**
   a. A great way to spend a weekend afternoon.
   b. A waste of time—I'd rather be watching TV or, if it's nice, doing something outdoors.

5. **Foreign films are . . .**
   a. Interesting—I'm up for seeing any movie, as long as the story sounds good.
   b. Too much work—all that reading.

6. **I'd rather spend money on . . .**
   a. A meal at a really nice restaurant.
   b. I wouldn't want to spend it—I'd rather keep it in an interest-bearing account.

If you and your LDP answered mostly A's, you'd probably enjoy playing tourist. If you're the LDP who's relocated, go ahead and be tourists together in your new hometown. Discover your new surroundings together: Go to a museum or restaurant you've heard about; get a map and walk the neighborhood; or just get lost—take no map and walk wherever your moods take you.

If you and your LDP answered mostly B's, schedule a day in bed. Turn off the ringer. Pretend you're on an island in the middle of nowhere, except that on your island, there are plenty of bad movies and junk food.

Thinking Outside the Standard Weekend-Visit Format

Mix things up once in a while to keep life exciting. LDPs have more options than close-range couples because of the potential for these types of visits:

■ **Meet at a halfway point.** It's even more fun when the halfway point is in the middle of nowhere. Book a room in a B&B for the weekend. You'll each have less distance to travel, and from that weekend on, the spot will be "your place."

■ **The surprise visit.** Coordinate with your partner's closest friend. Get the friend to take your partner out to dinner. Then show up at the restaurant or wait for her at her home with a huge bouquet.

Advice from Lifers: Military Wives on Visits

"We try different restaurants. We are usually meeting, either where he is ported or where I am for work. We go out and explore that new city together."
—Susie, Washington, D.C.

"Time together is precious. But surprisingly, the greatest comfort and the thing that gives the most joy is just being ourselves and being together. It's late nights watching bad movies on cable, talking over so much coffee you think you'll never sleep, holding hands while you walk down the street, going to a school program of the children, or sneaking away from work for lunch."

–Heidi, North Carolina

"I truly believe having him gone so much makes me appreciate him being home even more. The simplest of things seem that much better just having him home to enjoy it with me."

–Kristi, Washington, D.C.

You don't *really* know this person, but you know that you like her. You may have already spent an afternoon or evening with her, and talked to her on the phone or over e-mail—but now she's here, in your home, and you can't hang up the phone or say good-bye. She's not leaving for another 30 hours. What are you going to do with her?

■ **Plan many activities in advance.** Talk to her about what she likes to do and have several options up your sleeve in case circumstances beyond your control prohibit you from enacting your original plan. If you're planning outdoor activities, think of some indoor backup plans in case the weather turns foul. Try to account for mealtimes—planning a dinner at home or out, depending on logistics and your LDP's inclinations.

■ **Schedule time with friends (but not with family).** Thirty hours is a long time to spend alone with anyone. Break up all of that alone time by going out to dinner or drinks with some of your in-town friends. If you're the one visiting, you should insist on this; part of the mission of your visit is to get to know this person better. You can learn a lot about him from meeting his friends and seeing how he interacts with them. Keep family out of it, though, if it's still in the courtship stage. Meeting siblings or parents at this point may imply a seriousness that you don't feel. It may also make the other person feel undue pressure.

■ **Ask a sequence of "getting-acquainted" questions when it feels like the conversation is fizzling:**

1. What's your go-to karaoke song?

2. What book have you read that you think should be made into a movie?

3. Who would play you in the movie of your life?

4. Did you have any nicknames growing up?

5. Do you ever remember your dreams?

6. Did you have a pet growing up?

Don't just run down the list of questions, of course. Introduce them into the conversation at a logical time and place.

Washington, D.C., couple Mark and Eric went long-distance when Mark got a job in New York. They decided Mark would live in the city on his own for a while before they talked seriously about Eric moving to join him. They were dating for three years before the move and for another two and a half years after the move. Eric thinks they probably would've figured out earlier that they should break up had they spent their weekends more wisely. They didn't have any downtime. "We were always on the go," says Eric. "We didn't do what people who live in the same city do, which is veg out on the couch, hang out at home alone. We were always out with friends."

COUPLE CASE STUDY

Eric, 32, teacher, and Mark, 32, lawyer

Dependents/pets: 0

Distance: Washington, D.C., to New York City = 225 miles

L–D for: Two and a half years

Frequency of visits: Every weekend

Their advice: Schedule a set time to talk about the relationship and your feelings. Make these talks a priority.

Status at press time: Broken up

Meeting Your Significant Other's New Friends

Though it's important to schedule lots of together time during visits, it's also a good idea to meet your partner's new friends. Chances are, the person visiting has been hearing about all of these new people, but for one partner to feel a part of the other partner's life, they should meet and spend time with these new friends together.

See as much of your partner's "new life" as possible. Go to her office and meet her coworkers or meet some of her new friends for dinner or for drinks. It may be a little strange at first; adding a new person to the mix can change the dynamic, but can also provide everyone an opportunity to broaden their horizons. Just make sure you schedule plenty of quality alone time along with the socializing.

To make his LDP feel comfortable among all of his new friends, the host might consider laying the groundwork beforehand by:

■ Giving his LDP short, funny descriptions of each person she's going to meet, such as "Dan is the most anal guy in the office. Everything at his desk is lined up at right angles. He's obsessed with Diane, his secretary, but everyone pretends like they don't notice him staring at her all day." Or "Greg's the one who looks like he could be one of those hermits who lives in a cold-water shack in Montana—he's the one with the full mountain-man beard. But don't let the facial hair fool you. He's actually really outgoing."

■ Making flashcards complete with people's names spelled out phonetically as well as a few tidbits of info on each one—such as how he met them and what they do for a living.

Departures: Saying Goodbye

Usually one or both LD partners will begin to descend into a funk as early as the day before they have to say good-bye. After a few visits, it'll become obvious which of you becomes more distraught, when you begin to feel upset, and so forth—a pattern will emerge. Once it does, you can come up with suitable coping mechanisms. Here are some techniques to ease the departure.

#1: THE EVASION TECHNIQUE

■ Go out to dinner or drinks with friends the night before. While this may seem like "wasting a night" by not spending it as a couple, it may be better overall for your relationship. Experienced LDPs agree that being with other people will keep you distracted and shift your focus from that dreaded moment when you have to say good-bye.

■ A few hours before you're due to leave, go see a movie or play to keep your mind off of the impending good-bye.

■ Don't go to the airport/bus station/train station to see your partner off if you know you'll become too emotional.

#2: THE-YOU-CAN'T-GET-RID-OF-ME-SO-EASILY TECHNIQUE
■ Go to a photo booth and take pictures together so you'll have mementos from the visit.

■ Start planning your next visit: His place or yours? When? What will you do? Who will you see?

■ Leave little notes for your partner where he'll find them post-departure—either tucked into his bag or, if you've been visiting him at his home, taped to the milk in the fridge. Mention specific things you love about him or a private joke from the weekend.

■ Leave a phone message. Record a message on her answering machine while she's en route, so she'll get it when she gets home. Play one of "your" songs into her machine, or tell her what a great time you had with her.

#3: THE GOOD RIDDANCE TECHNIQUE

(Warning: not recommended by relationship counselors)

■ Allow yourself to become really annoyed with all of the little things your partner does, such as saying "Aaaah," after every sip of coffee or checking your shelf for dust before she puts her clothing away. Soon you won't be able to wait for her to leave.

■ Think about the joys of being alone at last, with no one to stare at you judgmentally while you sit on your couch in your underwear, eating marshmallow Fluff out of a jar.

Post-Departure Coping Strategies

"If you visit on the weekends, find something to do on Sunday night. Staying busy or being with people will help you deal after the other person leaves (which might be the worst feeling in the world)."—Mimi

To avoid sitting and thinking about how much you already miss your LDP, make plans to do something after he or she leaves.

■   Have a movie date with a good friend for that evening.

- Pamper yourself with a long hot bath or a lazy evening renting a movie and ordering take-out.

- Hit a bar and drown your sorrows in beer and darts.

- Sweat it out at the gym.

Sharpen your #2 pencils—it's time to take the VAT. Each LDP should answer the following questions without consulting the other. Compare your answers at the end. Give yourself a point for every answer the two of you answer the same way. Use the results to gauge whether or not you're in agreement. (See the scoring assessments after the VAT questions.)

1. **We see each other . . .**
   a. Just enough
   b. Not enough
   c. Way too much

2. **My partner's favorite thing to do on the weekend is**
   _____.

3. **My favorite thing to do on the weekend is _____.**

4. **True or false: I visit my partner more than he/she visits me.**

5. **My partner and I have sex . . .**
   a. Just enough
   b. Not enough
   c. Way too much

6. True or false: I wish that our visits consisted of more unscheduled, hanging-out-alone time.

7. True or false: We spend too much time hanging out with other people on our visits.

8. True or false: I'd like to spend more time during our visits socializing with others, going to museums, on hikes, and doing more scheduled activities in general.

9. Spending time at my partner's home/apartment/dorm room is like being:
    a. In a pig sty
    b. In an "after" photo in *Architectural Digest*
    c. In Pee Wee's playhouse
    d. Home

10. Our visits are . . .
    a. Routine and boring, and I like it that way
    b. Routine and boring, and I don't like it that way

Scoring: *8–10 points:* Don't change a thing. *6–8 points:* It may be time to make some changes. Do so, pinpointing the issues that came up in the questions you answered differently. *Less than 6 points:* It's time for a major visitation-routine overhaul.

Communication

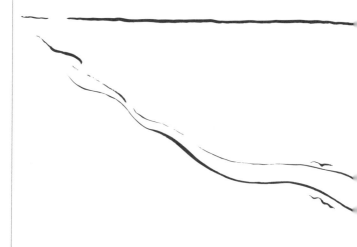

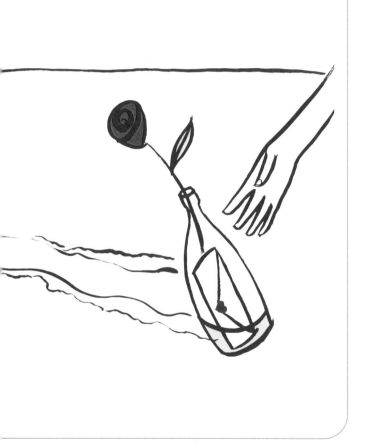

THE FOLLOWING MATHEMATICAL EQUATION SHOULD DRIVE HOME THE IMPORTANCE of communication in a long-distance relationship:

Zero physical contact + substandard verbal and written communiqués = an unsatisfying, short-lived relationship

The equation's as easy as $0 + 0 = 0$. (And you thought your grade-school math would never come in handy.) The first zero is the void that's left when you can't pop in to your partner's apartment after a horrible day at work for a reassuring hug. It's the delirium tremens (DTs) that set in a few days after your last visit and your last spoon. By whatever means possible, you must find some way to recreate the satisfaction of the perks that close-contact couples take for granted, and using good communication skills are the first, major step to making that second zero increase in value.

If your long-distance partner will only say "I love you" while gazing deep into your eyes, she'd better learn to get over her overwrought idea of romance. Fast. Because the LDP's most preferred method of delivering said intimacy is via telephone—you can hear your partner's voice and his deep breathing, and you can listen to him burping out your name after he downs a soda too fast.

Next in line as supplements to the phone call are snail mail (including care packages, love letters, and cards), e-mail, and all the other more high-tech communication gadgets: fax machines, videophones, and webcams.

Phone Protocol

How often and how long should phone conversations with your LDP be? That depends on your schedules and your phone stamina. You may agree to talk every night before you go to bed, say, around 10:00 P.M. If your schedule is too irregular to withstand a nightly call, you might want to leave the phoning "window" open for a longer period. Or, if you don't feel the need to talk every night, you can agree to talk every other day or every three days. The exact timing doesn't matter, as long as you both feel that you're getting what you need through regular, quality phone time. In fact, for most of the LDPs I spoke to, it's not the quantity of calls that's the problem, but the *quality*.

"The only way to maintain normalcy is to have short conversations but talk constantly so you feel like there's continuity."—Andrew

"S/He's Not a Phone Person"

Do men and women communicate differently? John Gray, the self-help guru behind the *Men Are from Mars, Women Are from Venus* franchise, and Dr. Lillian Glass, author of *The Complete Idiot's Guide to Understanding Men and Women*, both say that there are basic gender differences when it comes to communication. In a heterosexual relationship, they claim, a man and a woman should understand these differences in order to prevent fights and manage conflict resolution.

If their claim is true for regular relationships, then it's especially true in an LDR, when you don't have the benefit of the added context provided by a coded touch or glance. But assigning gender differences seems like a gross oversimplification. Although a man more frequently gets pegged as not being a "phone person," there are, of course, *women* who aren't good on the phone, and gay couples certainly don't follow the same gender pattern rules as straight couples. Inevitably, one partner in *any* couple is going to be a little less chatty when he's talking into a mouthpiece. Some people, according to psychologist Eric Levin, are just completely different in person than they are on the phone.

With that in mind, let's review some general communication glitches that can sabotage LDR phone conversations.

Recognize them. Then avoid them as best you can.

1. Sulking or pouting. When she senses you're in a funk and asks, "What's wrong?" do not, under any circumstances, reply "Nothing." Admit that your "nothing" is code for "pay attention to me." You may want her to cajole, to dig for the problem, or if she is the problem, to know exactly what she did to upset you—but you don't have the luxury to play these kinds of games in a long-distance relationship. Tell her what's wrong right off the bat.

2. Subpar storytelling skills.
Typical conversation:

> HER: "What did you do today?"
> HIM: "I went to work, came home, had some dinner. You?"
> HER: "Grocery shopping, fed the dog."
> HIM: "Oh, okay, good-bye."
> HER: "Bye. Sweet dreams."

On such exchanges, a long-distance relationship is not built. Get some details in there, some anecdotes. Did you make any observations during the day that you made a mental note of to tell your LDP later? Any funny stories from work, the commute home, the gym? Any problems that arose that you may need help with? If you find these hard to remember by the time you're actually on the phone, it may be helpful to carry around a pocket-sized notebook to jot things down as they occur during the day.

Here's an example of how a more satisfying conversation might start:

> HER: "Hey!"
>
> HIM: "Hey! I really couldn't wait to talk with you."
>
> HER: "I know! Me, too. I have to tell you what happened at work today."
>
> HIM: "Did you finally tell off your boss?"

3. Hogging the conversation and then hanging up before asking about your partner's day.

Example:

> HER: "Hi, so I *have to* tell you about this crazy thing that happened to me today at work. I was in the elevator and my boss came in and her skirt was stuck up in her pantyhose so all of the rest of us could see her underwear . . . [story goes on for another ten minutes] . . . and, oh my gosh, I have to

run. I'm late for poker night!"

HIM: "Oh, okay, well, uh—"

HER: "Talk to you tomorrow, honey." [Click]

This kind of exchange happens when the partner who is in a hurry and hardly has time to talk makes an obligatory call: She's calling because you agreed that you would talk daily, but she doesn't have time for a real conversation, so she's trying to squeeze a meaningful conversation into ten minutes.

If this becomes routine, it's a problem. Point it out and ask your partner not to call when it's clear she has no time to talk. And ask that when she does call, she makes a conscious effort to let you get a word in.

4. Forcing the you-suck-on-the-phone issue so much that it becomes a drain on the relationship.

If your partner really isn't a phone person, and that's not likely to change, perhaps he or she is a prolific writer. Make e-mail your regular mode of communication or, as suggested earlier, set up a phone date once every few days instead of talking to each other every day.

5. Worrying that there's not enough to talk about.

It may be that there's not enough news to impart when you're speaking every day—try speaking every other day or every three days. Or post this list of talking points next to your phone in case you continue to run out of topics:

- Where do you want to go on our next vacation?

- How's [family member/pet/friend] doing?

- What do you want for your birthday/the holidays?

- What's the worst date you ever had?

- Do you believe in God?

- Do you remember where you were when the *Challenger* exploded?

- Have you ever noticed how the local TV news teams make the tiniest storms sound really scary?

"Talk about the practical, day-to-day stuff during the phone conversations so your home time is reserved for dates, flirting, and time together that is not filled with adult responsibilities."–*Debbie, trucker's wife for 3 years*

Esther and Jonathan, who were L-D for more than a year, never ran out of things to talk about during their nightly conversations because they talked about everything and anything under the sun. "What kept it going was that we had stuff to talk about every day—abstract, philosophical things. Ninety-eight percent of why we stayed together had to do with the fact that these conversations were so consistently good," says Esther.

COUPLE CASE STUDY

Esther, 29, Ph.D. in comparative literature, and Jonathan, 28, lawyer

Dependents/pets: 0

Distance: Boston, MA, to Washington, D.C. = 450 miles

L-D for: A year and a half

Frequency of visits: Once a month for a three-day weekend; they also met at midway points for weekends.

Their advice: Have nightly phone calls. Send unexpected gifts.

Status at press time: Married and living in the same place

Phone Sex

"I can't talk about that. I'm at work!"—Megan A.

Can't quite get into aural sex? If your answer to that question is, "What? No! I'm the phone sex queen/king!"—go ahead and skip this section. But if you're the kind of girl who, when your partner calls and asks breathily what you're wearing, answers, "A pair of old sweats that I haven't washed in a couple months," read on.

Phone sex seems like a difficult hurdle for many to jump—it requires imagination, an adventuresome spirit, and most of all, a willingness to participate. Here are some methods to get you in the mood:

■ Before the phone call, work on your arousal techniques. If you can do it for yourself, on your own, you'll be more confident about becoming aroused while on the phone with your partner. Set aside some time, relax, and get to it. You may want to try imagining Brad Pitt or Britney Spears instead of your partner. (Carol Queen, co-owner of the San Francisco–based sex shop Good Vibrations, suggests trying out sex toys, like vibrators and lubricant.)

■ Practice talking tantalizingly to your reflection in the mirror, or to a pinup of your Hollywood crush. What to say? Think about what you enjoy when you are making love with your partner, and put that into words. Finish the following sentences: "I love it when you _____," and "It turns me on when you _____." You don't have to talk dirty—just practice letting your partner know exactly what you like. Once you've found the words, you can try them out during a phone call.

■ If you have a fantasy that you've never shared with anyone, try putting it into words. What do you think about when you get aroused? Describe it to your partner when he calls.

■ Try these openers—they're alternatives to the old standby, "What are you wearing?"

> ■ "I have this fantasy that I want to tell you about."

> ■ "Remember the time we . . ." (Remind him of an especially great sex moment from your shared past.)

> ■ "I wish you were lying next to me."

The Daily E-mail

"E-mail is important because you can feel close to the person, you can check in with them throughout the work day; just a quick note here or there to remind the person you're thinking about him."—Eric

The phone is a handy device for real-time conversations that foster connection, but it's not as useful as e-mail for firing off instant accounts of what just went down at your office or venting about something small and seemingly unimportant that you just have to get off your chest.

> "It's important to keep up the daily conversation, to talk about nothing, so you feel you're a part of each other's lives instead of always talking about the big issues."
> —Wendy

E-mail lets you vent in real time and pass along little observations that pop into your head throughout the day but which don't merit an actual phone call (unless you want to jot them down in a notebook and save them for a longer call to be made later). E-mail is also ideal for passing along logistics such as flight arrival and departure times, details of weekend plans, and other visit-related items that don't have to be decided right away.

Cher, an ex-LDP we met in Chapter 3, was not a fan of cyber-communication. She and her LDP e-mailed infrequently, and then only to exchange practical information. Cher felt that e-mailing all day would detract from their nightly phone calls. "E-mail is one of the worst things you can do in an LDR," she says. "It leaves room for so much misinterpretation, and the quality of a phone call at the end of the day before you go to sleep can't be replaced by quick quips made throughout the day over e-mail."

An interesting take, but most of the other LDPs I spoke with disagreed with Cher, pointing out that a relationship is built on details, and the little stuff is better communicated as it happens, not in retrospect. This lets your partner live your day with you in the moment and give you real-time advice.

Why You Shouldn't Fight Over E-mail

Ever heard of Internet flaming? That's when people get into nasty verbal swordfights in online chat rooms. It's easy to go from civil to confrontational when your adversary is invisible. For one thing, there's no voice inflection or body language to provide context, which means that a message can easily be misunderstood as accusatory or damning when it may have been meant as sarcastic or neutral. Such a misunderstanding can just as easily occur when you're e-mailing back and forth with someone you know very well. A sentence that is meant to be delivered with a raised eyebrow or a chuckle can be construed as confrontational, especially when the relationship is going through a difficult phase.

7 SIGNS YOUR E-MAILS ARE FLAMING

1. Your blood pressure is rising as you type, as evidenced by the reddening of your face and quickening of your breath.

2. The replies are getting so nasty, you gasp aloud upon reading them.

3. The replies are *so* nasty, you have to call your best friend and read them aloud to her so she can gasp, too.

4. The back and forth of messages is instantaneous—you might as well be on the phone. This indicates (a) that no one's counting to ten before hitting "send"; and (b) that both of you are so highly engaged that you're already anticipating your next comeback.

5. CAPS are creeping into the messages. You are now effectively YELLING at each other.

6. Emoticons went out the window two e-mails ago.

7. So did niceties such as writing each other's names at the beginning of each message and signing off with an "xo."

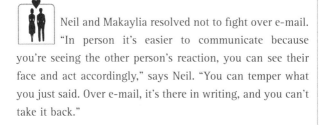 Neil and Makaylia resolved not to fight over e-mail. "In person it's easier to communicate because you're seeing the other person's reaction, you can see their face and act accordingly," says Neil. "You can temper what you just said. Over e-mail, it's there in writing, and you can't take it back."

≡ COUPLE CASE STUDY ≡

Makaylia, 28, lawyer, and Neil, 30, graphic designer

Dependents: 0

Pets: 2 cats

Distance: New York City to Villanova, PA = 104 miles

L–D for: One year

Frequency of visits: Every weekend

Their advice: Romantic gestures when you show up for a visit, like buying flowers for her when she picks you up at the train station, make the traveling part of the relationship seem less mechanical and more like courting.

Status at press time: Engaged and living in the same place

The Importance of Snail Mail

"At first the letter writing wasn't going well. He was an accounting major, a numbers person. His letters were few and far between. Eventually he got the hang of it. By the end of the semester I would get these great, long letters from him that he would write during accounting classes."—Brenda

Snail mail became endangered in the early 1990s, when it was replaced by e-mail as the go-to form of written communication. But for LDR purposes, handwritten letters—even well-chosen greeting cards—are an ace up the sleeve. They're unexpected, rare, and carry more weight, literally and figuratively, than a message that pops up on your screen. After all, your LDP went to the trouble to write on an actual piece of paper, slide it into an envelope, buy a stamp, and walk the whole thing over to a mailbox. To go to all of that trouble, this relationship *must* be special.

For those not familiar with the practice of letter-writing, here are some dos and don'ts:

- *Do* go to a quiet place to write.

- *Do* doodle in the margins, cross out words you've reconsidered—anything to make the finished document more a reflection of you, with all of your quirkiness and endearing imperfections.

- *Do* use colored pens.

- *Don't* be afraid to cross out your first attempt, toss it in the trash, and try again.

- *Don't* feel the need to write something serious just because putting pen to paper seems more permanent than e-mailing. Have fun with it.

"I write letters every night before falling asleep. I tell him everything that happened that day—how many loads of laundry I did to what the kids and I had for dinner. It helps to keep him up to date on what is happening. He keeps all the letters."—Kym

How to Write a Love Letter

Before putting pen to paper, think about what you want to convey. What's your message? It shouldn't be too general—e.g., you are my destiny and I love you (sweet, but boring). Make it unique. What made you think of writing a love letter to your partner in the first place—what was your inspiration?

If there was no one inspiration, when's the last time you thought of him or her? Where were you? What were you doing? What sparked your thoughts? If you miss her, what is it that you most miss about her? Did you see something that day that you thought was funny and wished she was there to share it with you? Get specific.

Here are some additional tips for writing an effective letter:

Avoid the generic opening, "How are you? I'm fine." Instead, start by explaining what you're thinking and feeling. For example: "Dear Emily, The bed seemed huge last night without you in it. I actually missed your snoring (you're totally cute when you snore) and the way your leg twitches and wakes me up."

Flowery language is unnecessary. Don't try to sound like Shelley or Shakespeare. Just write as you speak. The letter means more if it sounds like you.

Good:

"It's so sexy when you talk about hedge funds. Remember last time you were here and you were getting excited about fund performance and large investors and then we started making out on my couch?"

Bad:

"O Bob, Bob, wherefore art thou, Bob? Deny thy new job offer and refuse thy ambition, Or if thou wilt not, be but sworn my love, And I'll relocate to Peoria."

Add cologne or perfume to the letter, especially if there's one brand that you wear a lot and that your partner has admired. Try dabbing it (just a dab!) in the center of the letter page. If the perfume is in a spray bottle, hold the page six to eight inches away from the bottle, and spray. Beware—the effect can be strong and immediate. One LDP immediately booked a trans-Atlantic flight for a surprise visit because he was so entranced by his partner's scented letter.

"We sent a lot of letters. I bought special handmade paper, wax seals. They were over the top lovey-dovey. Jonathan drenched envelopes with cologne I had said I liked when we were with each other. We both kept our letters. We found them the other day when we were unpacking [after moving into a new house]."—Esther

Advice from Lifers: Military Wives on Communication

TIP #1: STAY IN TOUCH BY WHATEVER MEANS POSSIBLE.
"We talk to each other every night. We also invested in webcams for our computers. We can see each other while we are at our computers. Even if we don't chat with each other, it is comforting to see that other person just doing work or playing a video game."
—Susie, Washington, D.C.

"Deployments are routine, and e-mail and snail mail are often less than reliable. Phone calls are bi-weekly, and that's if the phone lines on the ship aren't too long. You rarely get a good connection with no echo or delay, and sometimes it cuts you off before you get the chance to say 'I love you.' We always say that first."

—Heidi, North Carolina

TIP #2: KEEP IT FRESH.

"I send him care packages every week. It helps me feel like I'm still taking care of him and it lets him feel closer to home by receiving stuff from me (stuff he can't get on the ship): food, candy, pictures, socks/underwear, pretty much anything he asks for."

—Kristen, California

"We send 'questions for couples' questionnaires to each other. It's amazing how much we learn about each other that way, even after seven years of marriage. Or I'll send a '20 reasons why I love you' note.

"When possible, we schedule phone conversations for when the kids are in bed so we can give each other that undivided attention. We send 'just saying hi' and 'I love you' or 'thinking about you' e-mails. We write plenty of letters back and forth, and I always send some erotic letters. He loves those!"

—Jill, North Carolina

TIP #3: PAY NO ATTENTION TO TIME ZONES.

"E-mail and webcams have really helped with this. I know one girl who turns her web cam on and leaves it on so if hubby gets on he can watch her sleep."

—Marci, Maryland

"Believe me, when he calls at three in the morning and you haven't heard his voice in weeks—you not only don't mind your sleep being interrupted, you are awake faster that you can say 'hello?'!"

—Heidi, North Carolina

"I always knew when the phone rang at 3 A.M. it was him. I always loved getting woken up by the sound of that phone ringing."

—Kristi, Washington

■ Write one word or one sentence on a postcard and send it to your partner. Send a new one every day. When read together, the words or sentences will add up to a special message.

■ Call your partner when you know she won't be home and play one of "your" songs, or a song that you've danced to or made out to, into her answering machine. It will make her smile when she comes home and plays her messages.

■ Send pictures, either in digital format or by snail mail, documenting your life for your partner. Photograph items large and small: your new flea-market find, the ink spot on your cat's stomach from when he sat on an uncapped pen, the lasagna you just made.

■ Buy a journal and write in it for a week. Include sections about how much you miss your partner and any funny things you saw that you wanted to share with her. Write everything from daily events to your hopes for the future—whatever is on your mind. At the end of the week, send it to your partner so that he can write in it for a week. Keep sending the notebook back and forth until you've filled every page.

Faxing, Videophones, and Webcams

Fortunately for the modern-day long-distance romance, there are plenty of gadgets and communication technologies that make it easier to be an LDP in the twenty-first century.

Faxing Fun

Think of it as speedy snail mail. Handwrite a short love note or a love letter that's a few pages long, and fax it to your LDP's home or workplace. Faxing is also a charmingly old-school way to send images, such as your face squished against the glass of a photocopier and transferred onto a piece of paper. See if he can recognize your squashed features. Or use the fax machine to send a ransom-note-style message, using letters and images you've cut out of magazines and pasted onto a page. Send a romantic fax by dispatching clip art of a single rose. (Even better, use this as a means to announce a later delivery of real, live roses.) Of course, only do these if there's no possible way the letter will be intercepted by a nosy coworker.

Another method is to disguise your personal fax to look like an official business-to-business memo, complete with a cover sheet and a typed letter on your letterhead. On the next two pages there's an example of this kind of "prank" fax.

To: Juanita Jones
From: Seymour Butts
Re: Agenda for three o'clock meeting

Ms. Jones,

It has come to my attention that we do not yet have an agenda for the meeting that is scheduled for this afternoon. Since we are scheduled to talk, generally, about our next visit, let me suggest several specific topics to better guide the discussion.

I would find it copasetic to go over the following issues:

1. The prospect of our going to see a movie, and if so, a list of preferences for which movie you'd like to see.

2. What kind of omelet you'd like me to make you on Sunday morning—Western, Spanish, or Greek?

3. The weekend's soundtrack—punk, singer/songwriter folkie, alternative, ambient techno?

4. How adorably rumpled you will look when you walk through my door Friday night, after three hours of traveling.

I would appreciate your quick turnaround on this matter.

Sincerely,

Seymour Butts

Seymour Butts

The Eye of the Beholder: Videophones and Webcams

When webcams first became available to the general public, a multitude of exhibitionists set up their own visual diaries online to allow the general public to watch them 24 hours a day. Hardly any of their activities were actually worth watching: Mostly they were doing mundane things like feeding their cat, reading a book, hanging out with friends, sleeping, or peeing. It may be difficult to get your head around exactly why anyone would want to watch a stranger do these things, but it's easy to imagine wanting to watch your LDP—if not for 24 hours a day, at least during the time you're talking to each other.

LDP USES FOR VIDEO CAMERAS AND WEBCAMS

- Play board games with each other.

- Gauge changes in your LDP's physical appearance, such as facial hair, highlights (and lowlights), and love handles.

- Put your kids in front of the camera for some quality time. (Kids can interact more easily through this visual mode of communication than they'd be able to on the phone.)

- Show progress made on crafty projects—a hand-knit sweater, a homemade bookcase, a decoupaged table top.

- Show off new material objects in your life—a pair of boots, clothing options for an upcoming event, techie gadgets, puppies, or a new belly-button pierce.

- Illustrate new injuries—a cut on your arm, the biggest mosquito bite you've ever had.

- Make funny faces at your LDP, making her laugh when she's down.

- And, of course, we'd be remiss without mentioning the potential for generating sexual arousal. Dress up as your LDP's favorite fantasy—Princess Leia? James Bond? Trinity from *The Matrix*?

c. 33rd century B.C.: Sumerians invent writing—allowing the first rays of hope for long-distance lovers.

1844: Morse sends a telegraphed message between Baltimore, MD, and Washington, D.C.

1866: Telegraph cable is laid across Atlantic Ocean. Now LDPs can communicate from one continent to another.

1860: The Pony Express is born, running through Missouri, Kansas, Nebraska, Colorado, Wyoming, Utah, Nevada, and California. On an average day, a Pony Express rider covers 75 to 100 miles. (He'd change horses at relay stations situated every 10 to 15 miles.) The first Pony Express mail, transported from St. Joseph, Missouri, to Sacramento, California, takes 10 and a half days. That may seem like a long time to wait for a letter, but back then it was considered an "instant message."

1876: Alexander Graham Bell invents and demonstrates the first telephone. Little did he know that the telephone would one day be cordless, and then portable, allowing callers everywhere to annoy other people on their bus or train who have no interest in hearing them talk to their LDPs.

1895: Guglielmo Marconi broadcasts the letter "S" in Morse code by radio.

1904: Reginald A. Fessender transmits speech by radio.

1918: U.S. Congress appropriates $100,000 to establish experimental airmail routes. The new service betters cross-country rail times by 22 hours.

1972: Ray Tomlinson sends the first e-mail using @ in the address.

1974: First personal computers are introduced.

1983: MCI places an order for 90,000 miles of fiber optic cable.

1991: The World Wide Web is born.

Life Between Visits

No MATTER WHAT TYPE OF LDR YOU'RE IN, "Between Time" will make up the bulk of it. If your "Together Time" outweighs your Between Time, your LDR cred is seriously low. Attempts to claim LDP status may be met with laughter from hard-core LDPs; but keep reading—there's helpful information in this chapter for you, too.

Surviving the time between visits is tricky, because it means adjusting to being alone when you've just been ensconced in intense couplehood. It's a little easier for couples who start out long-distance, since their home lives remain constant. Still, there's loneliness to contend with, especially during the days immediately following a weekend visit. Like a Band-Aid, your LDP is ripped away, and you—an open wound—are left to face the raw, harsh elements. That's perhaps a wee bit melodramatic—but you get the point.

The LDP Who Moves Away Versus the LDP Who's Left Behind

Nine out of ten of people left behind agree that it's worse to be the one who is left behind. Even though most of your local support system remains intact, your major source of support and companionship has just walked out the door, leaving you to go to all the usual places . . . alone. You're at home on Wednesday night watching *The West Wing* all alone. You're sitting at your neighborhood hangout, flanked by empty stools. Meanwhile, your partner is in some exotic new locale (even if it's remote, it's exotic, because it's new and unknown), seeing new sights and meeting new people and not thinking about you at all. Right?

Well, it's all a matter of perspective. Nine out of ten LDPs who move away agree that leaving your loved one behind is more difficult. Yes, there are new sights and new people to distract you from your misery for a few days, maybe even for a week. But then there's the inevitable night when you return home from your new job or your new school, slump down on your bed, and realize how lonely you are. You begin to really miss your old neighborhood, your old friends, and Smitty the bartender, who always mixes you a perfect apple martini. Suddenly, all of the newness seems completely superficial, and you'd trade it in a second to be back home again.

Bottom line: Both situations are equally hard. The best you can do is to try to cultivate your alone time, spend time with friends, and keep in close communication with your LDP during the long days between visits.

"Get busy living life the best way you can. Have fun every chance you get. Don't just sit home being depressed and letting life pass you by. There is more to life than just being with your man or woman!"—*Connie, trucker's wife for 29 years*

Get a Life
Making a home life for yourself that is well-balanced and

full is important for every LDP. "Have lots of friends and a life and lots of things to do on your own," advises relationship counselor Margaret Shapiro. Lean on your friends and family—the support system that's still in close range. And ensconce yourself in work or school. When Elizabeth left her husband in Washington, D.C., to pursue her Ph.D. in sociology in Austin, Texas, both were too busy with their demanding academic schedules—her husband was in med school—to think about how much they missed each other.

COUPLE CASE STUDY

Elizabeth, 31, professor, and Hugh, 31, doctor

Dependents/pets: 0

Distance: Washington, D.C., to Austin, Texas = 1,524 miles

L-D for: Three and a half years

Frequency of visits: Once a month at minimum

Their advice: Stay focused on your career and keep busy with your life. Take vacations together. "It helped that we were both students, so we could take a month together in the summer," says Elizabeth.

Status at press time: Married and living in the same place

If you're in school, take on some extra credits. If you're

working, stick around after hours to show your boss how hard you work. And follow some of these other tried-and-true techniques for LDPs who find themselves with a lot of time on their hands.

DO THINGS YOU WOULDN'T DO WITH YOUR PARTNER.

- Rent chick flicks/mindless action movies/foreign flicks—whatever kind of movie your LDP dislikes.
- Blare your favorite music—heavy metal? opera?—at full blast.
- Hog all the covers for yourself.
- Your LDP's allergic to peanut butter? Stock up on Skippy.
- Is she a health nut? Binge on junk food.
- Is he a junk food junkie? Purge those Mallomars from your cabinets and replace them with baked wheat crackers.

"I look back on that time fondly. I really missed him, but I began to enjoy spending time on my own. I began to enjoy my own company."—Wendy

SCHEDULE DIVERSIONS

- Sign up for a class you've always wanted to take—photography, tennis, street funk, klezmer appreciation.
- Get in some physical activity—a nature walk, a workout at the gym, some touch football, a yoga class.

- At the beginning of the week, schedule plenty of social activities—especially for the weekend if you're not going to be with your LDP. Check out museum shows or bookstore readings; find out whether your favorite team will be in town; go to that flea market you've wanted to check out.

- Volunteer—helping others will take your mind off of your own predicament and give you some perspective.

> **"If you are going to be gone a lot on the weekends, try to make plans with your friends during the week. It sucks if you find yourself in town one weekend going, 'Hmm, who do I go out with?'"**—Mimi

CULTIVATE IN-TOWN FRIENDSHIPS

- Being in a couple often means spending less time with your single friends. If you're the one left behind, renew the friendships that you've let go by the wayside.

- If you're in a new city, ask one of your new colleagues or a neighbor if they'd like to go for coffee or catch a movie.

- Organize a book group with friends and acquaintances.

- Throw yourself a housewarming party and invite new neighbors and work friends.

 "It can be very lonely sitting at home, so jump in the truck and go with him!"—*Donna, trucker's wife for 4 years*

133

Here are some schadenfreude-worthy flicks in which lovers come up against obstacles greater than distance. Watch these films and thank your lucky stars that you're in an LDR rather than any of these situations.

AN AFFAIR TO REMEMBER (1957) Dashing Cary Grant and glamorous Deborah Kerr fall in love on a European cruise, but both are engaged to others. They agree to meet at the Empire State Building in six months. Madness and miscommunication ensues!
Obstacles to overcome: Already committed fiancés, miscommunication, a crippling injury.

ROMEO AND JULIET (1968) You know the story. The Franco Zeffirelli–directed version, starring Olivia Hussey as Juliet, is particularly heart-wrenching and beautiful.
Obstacles to overcome: Dueling families, nosy nurses, a potion-happy friar, a tendency for long-winded monologues.

MANNEQUIN (1987) A young artist (Andrew McCarthy) gets a job designing department store windows and creates a beautiful mannequin (played by a pre-*Sex and the City* Kim Cattrall). She's so exquisite, he falls in love with her. Problem is, she's a mannequin.
Obstacles to overcome: Only the artist can see her as she truly

is; others see only a lifeless piece of wood. Their fleeting dates must occur during the short periods of time when she comes alive.

BEFORE SUNRISE (1995) Ethan Hawke plays Jesse, an American who has traveled to Europe to meet up with his girlfriend. After "a long overdue meltdown," Jesse leaves the girlfriend to board a train to Vienna and catch a cheap flight home. On the train he meets Celine (Julie Delpy), a beautiful Frenchwoman who is returning to Paris. Jesse tells Celine his sad story, adding that "the long-distance thing never works." (He'll be burned by those very words in short order.) He convinces Celine to get off the train with him so they can spend a day together in Vienna. Day turns to night, and the young couple spends 14 hours talking. After discovering that they're both really, really deep, it's time to part ways. Will they ever see each other again?

Obstacles to overcome: Self-involvement, the couple's tendency to converse at length about nothing, his anti-LDR stance, an ocean.

DANGEROUS BEAUTY (1998) In fifteenth-century Venice, Marco (Rufus Sewell) falls in love with beautiful, brilliant Veronica (played by Catherine McCormack) but cannot marry her because of their class differences—he is high-born but she's from questionable stock. So she steels herself and becomes a courtesan—

one of the best in the city. She influences politics using her potent effect on men, but the man she really wants to be with is out of her reach.

Obstacle to overcome: A strict hierarchical society, war, infidelity, rows and rows of tiny buttons.

YOU'VE GOT MAIL (1998) Kathleen (Meg Ryan) owns a children's bookshop whose very existence is threatened when Joe (Tom Hanks) opens a huge chain bookstore in this remake of *The Shop Around the Corner* (1940). Though they hate each other in real life, they get hot and heavy online, under aliases. When Joe finds out that his cyber-girlfriend is actually Kathleen, he has to decide whether or not to reveal his true identity.

Obstacles to overcome: A business rivalry, the rise of the corporate superstore, the uncertainty of cyberlove, a tenuous onscreen chemistry that hasn't been the same since *Joe Versus the Volcano (1990).*

A VERY LONG ENGAGEMENT (2004) An epic long-distance love story about a young woman's search for her fiancé, who may or may not have been killed in World War I.

Obstacles to overcome: Graphic battle scenes, excruciating suspense, plot twists galore.

Advice from Lifers: Military Wives on Life Between Visits

TIP #1: KEEP BUSY.

"I am a workaholic. I work *a lot*, probably a little under 100 hours a week. I enjoy my work immensely, and I find great satisfaction in it."

—Susie, Washington, D.C.

"Me and my kids survive by living life! We go to ball games and buy hubby a ball cap and send him our ticket stubs. We send him spelling tests or essays that received high marks, and photographs of us in every place we go. We make lists of things we want him to see or do with us upon his homecoming. We send postcards when we visit someplace out of the way. We send care packages to Dad with his favorite things. The kids usually send silly stuff like plastic soldiers, squirt guns, McDonald's toys, or anything they think will make him smile."

—Heidi, North Carolina

"Stay active with things you *have* to do. What I mean is I would find things such as going to work, going to college, making a commitment to an activity that I had to see through so I couldn't get depressed and stay home and feel sorry for myself."

—Marci, Maryland

TIP #2: STOP THINKING ABOUT YOUR LDP AND START THINKING ABOUT YOURSELF.

"I've learned that 'me time' is important. Read a book, take a bath, get a haircut, get my nails done. It helps me keep my sanity.

"I'm not superwoman and no one expects me to be. I have learned to ask for help—whether that means asking someone to help me with my yard work or to watch the kids so I can run errands."

—Jill, North Carolina

TIP #3: A GOOD ATTITUDE HELPS. SO DO MOTIVATIONAL POSTERS.

"Mentally, I try to keep a positive attitude. I have a poster that I made that reassures me and gives me support that reads, 'The separation is temporary, the commitment is forever.' This helps me to remember on the bad days that I can get through this and that the reward is my husband coming home.

"If we don't know how long he will be gone, I will have

a calendar to count down the days gone. It has the saying on it 'With every day away, we are one day closer to home-coming.'"

—Kym, Wisconsin

TIP #4: LEAN ON OTHERS.

"I have a large support network of friends and family in the area with whom I do things all the time. They are there to lend a shoulder when I need one to cry on."

—Susie, Washington, D.C.

Keep the Flame Lit

Don't get so focused on keeping yourself busy that the method works too well and you forget about your LDP. Work into your busy schedule enough time to call your LDP, shop for surprise gifts, and write love letters. Snail mail, greeting cards, and phone sex, all of which are covered in Chapter 4, are important, but expected. There are more creative ways to remind your LDP of your existence.

The gestures for which you go that extra mile benefit your relationship in many ways: You win points for being romantic. Plus, your LDP is instantly reminded of how fantastic you are and how remiss she was in looking twice at the cute, new office intern.

On the following pages, you'll find guidelines that you should feel free to personalize. For your care package, think of specific moments that you've shared. How can you recreate these—in a box? There may be songs that have special meanings for you and your LDP—put these on a mix CD. As for the feng shui cure, well, a little Eastern mysicism never hurt any relationship.

Make Care Packages

"Six months into it, Jonathan sent me two Tiffany's boxes—one had a pearl pendant and the other was pearl earrings—to celebrate six months together."—Esther

Nothing says love like a special delivery from your LDP. Gifts have more meaning when you're in a long-distance relationship because they stand in for the intimate moments that close-range partners take for granted.

If your partner isn't the creative type, request that she simply attempt some romantic gestures. If she's worried she'll disappoint, assure her it's the thought that counts. Try showing her what you want and need by doing it yourself. Here's a list of creative gifts that will tell your partner you're thinking about her. They don't have to be expensive—a box full of cheap, funny gifts is sometimes preferable.

"He sent flowers to me at work a lot. I got a reputation for always having flowers in my office."—Megan C.

- If you are the one who was left behind, send your partner a package that reminds her of home: the local (nonperishable) food she loves, a copy of the hometown newspaper, a picture of your apartment, and snapshots of some of the favorite places the two of you used to go to together.

- Send digital or hard copy photos of your garden on the day it sprouts tulips, of your cat doing something funny, of you with your new haircut, of the new wart on the back of your wrist.

- Order one of those jigsaw puzzles, mugs, magnets, or pins that you can print with a picture of yourself.

- Carry around a tape recorder over the course of one or two days. Make a tape to tell your partner about your day, what you're doing, sights you're seeing, sounds you're hearing, scents you're smelling—and how much you miss her. Send it to her, along with one of your T-shirts spritzed with your cologne.

- Send him a plane, train, or bus ticket for the next time he's planning to visit.

- Make coupons with promised tasks—good for a backrub, a home-cooked meal, a sexual favor—to be cashed in during the next visit.

- Buy your partner a $50 phone card.

- If you can't be together on holidays, send a themed care package. For the 4th of July, pack up a picnic basket complete with plastic ants and sparklers. For Halloween, throw together some of her favorite candy, some silly string so she can play tricks on her coworkers, and an action heroine mask.

- Make a mixed tape or CD. Decide on a theme, then create a playlist. Throw in some of his favorite songs as well as some songs that mean something to you as a couple. Use the suggestions on the following pages to inspire you.

LDR STATEMENT SONGS:

"Crazy"/Patsy Cline

Statement: I'm crazy with loneliness. And feeling just a little bit country.

"Blue"/Joni Mitchell

Statement: I want to express my love by knitting you a sweater, shampooing your hair, and doing other fun couple stuff.

"I'm So Lonesome I Could Cry"/Hank Williams

Statement: I'm feeling pathos. These sad lyrics—a lonesome whippoorwill, a falling star, a weeping moon—are even sadder because they're sung by Hank, a promising young singer whose career was cut tragically short.

"All I Have to Do Is Dream"/Everly Brothers

Statement: It's a little obsessive how much I'm thinking about you. I can't get you out of my mind. I realize that this is a little creepy—but isn't it sweet, too?

"Please Mr. Postman"/The Marvelettes

Statement: Slacker! Get off your lazy butt and write me a letter, e-mail me, call me. C'mon, already! I'm waiting.

"Take the Last Train to Clarksville"/The Monkees
Statement: Just like the couple in this song, I'd love to meet you at a halfway point and spend a night together.

"Love Rollercoaster"/Red Hot Chili Peppers
Statement: This song's metaphor aptly reflects the ups and downs of our LDR, even if the couple in the song isn't necessarily in an LDR. Also, the profanity and sexual content herein indicate that I'm feeling a little saucy.

"Right Here Waiting"/Richard Marx
Statement: I feel much like this lonely man who, in the moodily lit video for this song, is sitting at his piano, his hair bushy and unruly like a lion's mane. Like him, I despair over the distance between us. At times I wonder how we'll ever make it—but I know that we will. Oh baby, we will.

"It took a few years for me to get used to him being gone most of the time. I was wondering what was the point of being with a man that was never home with me. But through the years, you learn to deal with it. I still miss him, but I am just used to it now. Don't know how or when it happened. But thank God it has!"—*Diane, trucker's wife for 13 years*

Enact a Feng Shui "Cure" on Your Home

Feng Shui experts not only provide advice on how to set up your apartment or house for maximum happiness, good health, and success in all aspects of your life, they also provide "cures" that focus on specific areas.

The "marriage cure" is intended to encourage the longevity and happiness of an existing relationship. This is a good exercise for when your partner is not around.

Here's what you'll need:

1. A picture of yourself and a picture of your partner. The two pictures should be about the same size.

2. A long red ribbon or string, all in one piece. The ribbon should be at least 100 times the length of the pictures.

3. A red envelope that's big enough to fit both photos inside.

Perform the cure:

1. Write your full name and the word "matrimony"—or, if you're not ready for marriage, "love"—on the back of your partner's picture. On the back of yours, write your partner's full name and the same word.

2. Under the light of a full moon, tie the pictures together: place them face-to-face and wrap the red ribbon around them 99 times.

3. Accompany the act with positive visualization, picturing yourself and your partner as perfect soul mates.

4. Put the photos in the red envelope and sleep with it beneath your pillow for nine consecutive nights.

5. On the tenth day, throw the envelope into moving water, such as a river or ocean that is strong enough to carry the envelope away.

Apart Together: Devising Long-Distance Rituals

We've already established that a major drawback to LDRs is that they lack the sharing of day-to-day stuff, such as going to the movies, cooking dinner together, and splashing water on each other when you're doing the dishes. To fill this void, you may want to come up with rituals you can do over the phone or long-distance.

LDPs can remain connected through creative ways, little gestures that keep you intimate and connected. These are the puffs of oxygen that reignite the fire and compensate for all of the relationship benefits you're not getting. Without them, an LDR might wither and die. Here are a few:

- Call first thing in the morning to tell your LDP how much you miss him.

- Have a TV show that you watch together, each of you

cradling the phone in your neck and giggling and crying together when appropriate. Or, if the phone bill precludes staying on the phone this long, make a date to call each other after the show and analyze it plot point by plot point.

- Go to the same movie or rent the same movie on the same night—call each other afterward to talk about it.

- Arrange for lunch from her favorite restaurant to be delivered to your LDP either at work or home. (Consult with a friend or coworker beforehand to make sure it's not a day she has a lunch date scheduled.)

- Call in to his favorite radio station and dedicate a song to him when you know he'll be listening.

- Send each other compatibility questionnaires (easy to find online if you search under "compatibility questionnaire") and discuss your results, question by question.

- Send each other tacky postcards with cryptic messages written on the back.

- Meet up and flirt in chat rooms under aliases that you've agreed upon.

When the Cat's Away . . .

One major drawback to not being in close proximity to your partner is not being *entirely* sure that your partner is not making eyes at an attractive man or woman who's closer to home. All you have to go on is what she's telling you over the phone, and even in the most trusting relationship, that little nagging feeling of "Is that friend really just a friend?" can blow up into full-blown jealousy.

You owe it to yourself and your relationship to get these feelings out in the open. Issues regarding monogamy, exclusivity, and flirtation crop up in all relationships, but they carry an even heavier weight for LDPs because the room for misunderstanding and misinterpretation is directly related to the physical distance between you.

Monogamy

"The fundamental values in a relationship are trust, love, and respect for another person, and you won't have that if you're seeing other people."—Cher

Let's face it. Loneliness is hard. There's temptation, especially when you're surrounded by people closer to home with whom you can share your favorite pastimes, hobbies, experiences, and day-to-day venting. But trust is key, just as it is for close-range relationships. You need to trust your partner. You can't be sure who she's seeing all day, every day, nor should you want to keep such close tabs on her.

Trust can develop only when you deal with the issue of monogamy and exclusivity head-on. Relationship counselors agree that monogamy is the only option for an LDR that's going to last. They suggest talking together or with a therapist to face the likelihood that temptation, jealousy, or doubts may happen *before* any suspicions arise. Ask yourself, "What will we do?" and discuss it with your partner. And if it turns out that one of you wants to see other people, it may be better to break up altogether.

One LDP who tested the waters confessed to her partner that she'd gone on a few dates with someone and had kissed him a few times. She admitted she had made a mistake. She and her LDP took a month off from the relationship, but when they got back together, her partner cheated on her. The episode taught her this lesson: Once one of you violates the other's trust, it's very difficult to get it back.

Flirtation

"You have to trust the person. By putting restrictions on your partner, by making threats, it'll make them more defiant; you have to say, I trust that person and I'm not going to question them."—Wendy

LDPs exist in a strange gray zone between "single" and "married." You don't fit in with your married friends, but you don't quite fit in with your single friends, either. You don't have your partner around to accompany you to couples' outings, and your single friends might be preoccupied with going out on the town, looking for love. Chances are you feel more comfortable with the singles. After all, you can't summon your significant other to be your better half for a couples' night, but you probably remember how to go out, have fun, and flirt.

It all comes down to trust, says one relationship counselor, who advises that LDPs make more friends and create more opportunities—through volunteering or taking classes—to connect with people in atmospheres that aren't pick-up scenes, so that the temptation to flirt is minimized.

Reduce your partner's temptation to stray by continuing to communicate with her as much as possible. Don't let two or three days slip by because you're busy. At least make time for a short phone call. Many times an affair begins as a friendship, but if you and your partner remain best friends, he or she won't feel the need to foster that companionship with someone else. Studies show that one reason people cheat on their partners is because the intimacy has left their relationship. Try to maintain a steady level of intimacy with your LDP by putting your relationship first, sending digital pictures, love letters, and making time not only to speak on the phone but also to see each other in person.

Every LDP will likely encounter temptation at some point—it's pretty much a given. But so long as each LDP retains a sense of commitment and open communication, you and your partner will be able to contend with it.

It's possible that your LDP has a close male or female friend where he or she lives—someone with whom she goes to movies, out to dinner, or to parties, work functions, and other events you'd be attending if you lived nearby. Having this "stand-in" is natural. There are voids that need to be filled when in a long-distance relationship: day-to-day companionship is the most immediate. There are also the random events that crop up that you don't want to do alone: work events for which you need an escort, the half-price movie night you like to go to every Wednesday, the new mall you want to check out two towns over. Here's how to assess whether that stand-in is turning into a replacement.

Top Ten Signs Your LDP May Be Straying

1. He starts telling lots of stories that feature the stand-in, e.g., "Amanda and I were walking to class today"; "Amanda said the funniest thing today."

2. She starts constantly quoting her good friend's opinions—"Well, *Dudley* says a meteor's *definitely* going to collide with Earth in 2041"—and/or telling jokes that are not typical of her sense of humor.

3. Instead of having two or three friends who are on a rotation for escorting duties, he brings the same person to all events.

4. She mistakenly says the stand-in's name when she means to say yours, or even worse, while you're having sex.

5. He starts assigning her attributes to you, e.g., "I thought you were *left*-handed," or "I thought you hated broccoli?"

6. She generally calls less, e-mails less, and is less excited about visits.

7. He's less than eager to set up an introduction between you and the stand-in.

8. He's disinterested in sex.

9. She suddenly has passionate new interests—in music, movies, food, etc.—that seem to be influenced by one person.

10. You find out that he's been asking the stand-in for advice about problems you're having in your relationship.

Dealing with Naysaying Friends and Family

"I just stopped talking to them about Jonathan. They'd ask about him, and I'd say he was fine and then change the subject."—Esther

All LDPs face the external pressure applied by friends, family members, and other buttinskis who are subtly or not so subtly cheering for you to abandon your geographically undesirable relationship. These naysayers commonly come out of the woodwork during the times between visits, when you're most vulnerable.

To be fair, the friends and family members who seem negative about your LDR are only providing what they consider necessary—a reality check. They have only the best intentions. They see that you're struggling with loneliness between visits, and that the relationship is a huge time-suck and money-suck, and they wonder if it's really worth it. You may want to use this opportunity to talk about your situation with someone who knows you really well. What may make listening to them difficult is that they're probably echoing the nagging voice inside your head that's been asking the same questions.

"My roommates in grad school would tell me, 'You should date other people. He'll never know.' You just have to push that away and know that what you want is right."-Erica

This is why you might be tempted to respond with sarcasm—"What? It's going to be hard? I didn't even think of that!"—instead of attempting to engage in meaningful dialogue. But the straightforward approach is more effective: "I know it's going to be hard, but I really believe in this relationship, and I want to try and make it work. What I really need from you now is your support."

If you happen to meet other LDPs in your town with whom you get along, try to connect with them so you can commiserate with people who are in a similar situation. As for your other friends, let them know that you need their support in general, then copy down the letter on the following pages (filling in the correct names) and give it to them so they will know how to behave.

"My friends and family all told me how crazy they thought I was . . . after we got married."—Megan A.

Dear [friend's name here],

First let me start by saying that I truly appreciate your concern for me and my situation. I know that you have my best interests in mind. With that said, let me assure you that I know what I'm doing. I wouldn't be putting myself through all of the suckiness that goes with being in an LDR if I didn't truly believe that I wanted to be with [name of LDP].

So, the next time you're about to drop a strong hint that I should abandon [name of LDP] simply because [name of LDP] doesn't live in the same town, please consult the following list and choose a more supportive conversation topic:

- Ask me how our last visit went.
- Ask me when we're going to see each other next.
- Ask me how I'm doing and how it's going in general.
- Ask me if I've read any good books lately.

Please do not:

- Try to set me up with anyone else.
- Point out hotties I should flirt with when we're out at a bar or a party.
- Call my LDP "what's-her-name."
- Clip articles for me that chronicle the negatives of LDRs.

And if I ever do indicate that things are not going so well for me and my LDP, please do not do any of the following:

- Jump up and clap your hands together gleefully.
- Pull out your cell phone and start dialing the person you've been wanting to set me up with.
- Exhale deeply and say, "Finally, you've come to your senses."

If you follow the guidelines in this letter, I promise to stop screening your calls.

Sincerely,

[your name here]

Handling Emergencies When You're Apart

The times when you really need your partner can be especially challenging when he or she is far away. It's difficult to handle the bad stuff alone—everything from a bad day at work to dealing with a death in the family—when you're used to having a partner to help you through. Make sure you have some way of getting in touch with your LDP at all times. Each of you should have a cell phone. And if you should have difficulty reaching your LDP, be absolutely sure that you have contact numbers for people who are in close contact with your LDP locally.

Make a phone list like the one below so that you can get information to your LDP in case of a real emergency:

	NAME	PHONE #
Best friend		
Sibling		
Parent		
Roommate		
Neighbor		
Coworker		
Landlord		

Todd and Erica met at Penn State, where she was a year ahead of him. They started dating at the beginning of her senior year, and by the time she graduated, they had decided to stick it out. They stayed together, through her time in grad school and even as he and she both bounced around the East Coast for their respective careers. One sticking point in their LDR was Todd's lack of a cell phone. "He didn't have one for the longest time," recalls Erica. That made it hard for her to get in touch with him. "Stupid stuff would happen to upset me," she says, "and I would want to talk to him. I'd be trying to track him down. It was hard because he'd be the only person I wanted to talk to."

COUPLE CASE STUDY

Erica, 27, journalist, and Todd, 27, fitness coach

Dependents/pets: 0

Distance: Pittsburgh, PA, to State College, PA, and Fairfax, VA = 136 and 250 miles; then, Raleigh, NC, to Fairfax, VA = 250 miles

L–D for: Three and a half years

Frequency of visits: Varied from once a week to once a month

Their advice: Have faith it's going to work and that this is the person you want to be with forever.

Status at press time: Living in the same city and just celebrated their sixth anniversary

The Future

IF YOU'VE MADE IT THIS FAR—PAST THE MEETING AND COURTSHIP PHASES, the visits, the time between the visits—you will be very tempted to stay in your LDR, even if it's not really working out. After all, not staying in it would mean you've wasted all of that time, effort, and money and that all of those emotional ups and downs were for naught.

Newsflash: These are not good reasons for staying in a relationship. All relationships, whether long-distance or close-range, need to be assessed on the same merits of whether, truly, you and your partner can go the distance. Inertia—where one or both of you are too comfortable in the present to think about or plan for the future—might be a sign that the relationship doesn't *have* a future.

At some point you'll need to talk about the fact that one of you is going to have to move. Because the stakes are higher in an LDR—you don't want to uproot yourself and end up breaking up with the person after a few months—you'll really need to put some thought into the relationship's staying power. "Have a strong gut feeling," advises Robin Gorman Newman, founder of www.lovecoach.com. "Make sure it's mutual, that there's an equal investment." Like any other relationship, she advises, yours has to be able to stand the test of time.

Of course, while time is passing, there are other tests you can perform.

This chapter includes several relationship assessment tools to help you figure out whether this is an LDR worth staying in. Once that decision is made, it will be time to come up with a plan for the future. Just be sure that you're not making this decision in a vacuum: Share your thought process and observations with your LDP at all times.

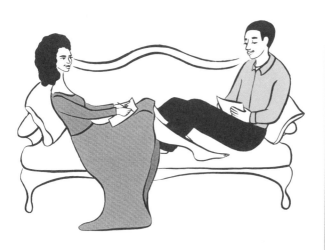

1. **When you and your partner are asked to tell the story of your romance, you . . .**
   a. Agree on most points.
   b. Have different stories about how it happened.
   c. Don't really remember.

2. **You decided to go full-speed ahead with the LDR that you're in because . . .**
   a. He/she is the love of your life.
   b. You haven't found anyone closer to home, so why not?
   c. You find same-place relationships stifling.

3. **You feel like you and your LDP are . . .**
   a. In agreement about your level of commitment.
   b. Not in agreement—one of you wants more of a commitment than the other.
   c. You don't know. You've never talked about how casual or serious you are.

4. **When you and your LDP are visiting each other you . . .**
   a. Want to do the same things.
   b. Disagree on some things, but can usually find a happy compromise.

c. Argue about almost everything—where to eat, when to wake up, who to go out with, which movie to see.

5. **When you and your LDP are apart . . .**

   a. You're satisfied with the frequency with which you communicate.

   b. You often wonder why your LDP isn't making more of an effort to connect.

   c. You don't really talk or write much, but you don't really want to, so it's okay.

6. **When you're not with your LDP, most of your time is spent . . .**

   a. Keeping busy with work and friends.

   b. Half and half—keeping busy and pining.

   c. Pining for your LDP.

7. **As far as sex goes, you and your LDP . . .**

   a. Are in total agreement.

   b. Have some issues, but who doesn't?

   c. Disagree: One of you definitely wants to be having it more, not to mention more creatively.

8. **Since you've been in your LDR, you've . . .**
   a. Been attracted to other people but never acted on it.
   b. Kissed someone but instantly regretted it. Hey, you were lonely.
   c. Cheated on your LDP more than once. It's okay, though—you're pretty sure she's cheating on you, too.

9. **As far as your LDP's day-to-day life, from his work to his family and friends . . .**
   a. You're very familiar with his or her daily routine and current "issues."
   b. You know what your LDP does and the names of his friends, but not a lot of the details.
   c. You don't even know what he does for a living.

10. **You and your LDP . . .**
    a. Have a plan for the future.
    b. Know that, theoretically, one of you will eventually have to move to be with the other, but you're not sure who, where, when, or how.
    c. Have never talked about the future.

11. If your LDP's birthday were tomorrow . . .

    a. You'd know exactly what you'd get for him or her—you've had your eye on something special for a while.

    b. You'd get him or her a gift certificate or flowers.

    c. You'd call and wish your LDP a happy birthday and maybe send an e-card.

RESULTS:

Mostly A's: You and your LDP are built to last. According to relationship experts, you've done all the right things—from defining your relationship to keeping the lines of communication open to coming up with a plan for the future.

Mostly B's: Your LDR is a little lackluster. See, the whole thing with LDRs is that they require much more effort, time, and consideration than a regular close-range relationship, so if you want this to last, you may want to step it up a bit. Start by having some honest, open talks with your LDP about where you are and where you're going.

Mostly C's: You call this a relationship? Ha!

Red Flags: Signs It's Not Going to Last

"He backed out on my moving in with him. He went from saying, 'Well of course we'll live together' to me saying, 'Would it be better if I got my own place?'"
—Jennifer

This type of waffling is a Big Red Flag that the relationship is shifting—and not for the better. Here are some other signs. If you notice two or more of the following, your relationship may be doomed.

- One of you becomes fidgety and way too focused on finding "alone time" when you're together longer than a weekend.

- One of you wants marriage and kids; the other doesn't.

- One LDP isn't making as much time for the relationship.

- One LDP (the one who's moved away) doesn't want to introduce the other to his new friends or bring her to his office to meet his coworkers. (He should be eager to show her off and have his new friends get to know her.)

- When asked why you're staying together, you reply, "Well, we've made it this far." (As mentioned earlier, you should never stay in a long-distance relationship just to make all of the blood, sweat, and tears worth it.)

- You're willing to move to be with your LDP, but your LDP doesn't want you to.

- Your LDP says she wants you to move to be with her, but she's not looking for a different space for the two of you, or investigating job opportunities for you, or making room in her apartment for you.

Adam and Jennifer were together for a total of six years, five of which were spent long distance. The two started out relatively close-range, in D.C. and Baltimore, but Adam's job, as a TV news producer, meant he was constantly switching markets—and states. He lived in Maryland, South Carolina, Michigan, Maine, and Washington during the five years they were long distance. Jennifer decided to leave D.C. and move to Seattle after falling in love with the city during her visits there; she was also ready for a job change. Finally, Adam was living somewhere where she could see herself moving. About six months after she moved to Seattle, Adam cut bait, deciding he didn't want to be in the relationship anymore. The first thing Jennifer did was get a cat. (Adam was allergic to cats.)

=== **COUPLE CASE STUDY** ===

Jennifer, 35, writer/editor, and Adam, 35, TV news producer

Dependents/pets: 0

Distance: Washington, D.C., to Baltimore, MD; Columbia, SC;
Portland, ME; Detroit, MI; and Seattle, WA = 45, 483, 539, 524
and 2,763 miles, respectively

L–D for: Five years

Frequency of visits: Every one to two months

Their advice: Be cautious before you quit your job and move.
Look for signs that the LDP you're moving to be with wants you
there. You may want to do a trial run or plan an extended visit
after you make the decision to move, but before you start putting
the gears in motion, just to make sure this is what you both want.

Status at press time: Broken up

Signs You'll Go the Long Haul

The key here is to assess your compatibility. Take a step back
and look at your relationship with an analytical eye. Here are
some quick and painless exercises to help you do so.

Make Three Lists

1. Pretend you're single again and make a list of the traits
you'd want in a potential partner.

2. Now write down your real-life partner's top ten positives.

3. Compare the two lists. How much do they have in common—enough so that you feel comfortable saying this person is The One? Or so little that you feel you might be settling?

4. Now look at the list of your partner's best traits and ask yourself, "Are these traits that I recognize in myself?" This could be a good indicator of your compatibility. Though the "opposites attract" theory has been around since post–World War II (when social scientists first began to research married couples to find out who was attracted to whom and why), it's becoming more widely believed that the couples who last actually have quite a bit in common.

5. Make a list of ten negative traits that your partner has. Which list was easier to write? Do the negatives outweigh the positives or vice versa?

6. Burn the lists. (You may think it's okay for your partner to see the positives list, and it will be—until they ask, "Is there a negatives list, too?")

"Work, work, work at it. Commit to making it work. Every day, think of your marriage and your lives together before you think of yourselves. Think of yourselves as a couple first, then as individual people." *–Kris, trucker's wife for 6 years*

Analyze Your Oral History

Psychologist John Gottman reported to the American Psychological Society in June 1995 that by listening to the oral histories of 52 couples, he could predict with a 94 percent accuracy rate which of them would stay together. With this in mind, the next time someone asks how you met, notice how the two of you recount the story. (You could even ask a friend to pose the question next time you're together so that you can play social scientist.) Here's how to read between the lines.

SIGNS OF A HEALTHY RELATIONSHIP:

1. Recalling details with fondness; for example: "He was wearing this adorable blue shirt that brought out the blue of his eyes," or "He was so chivalrous. He held open every door."

2. Making a short story long or embellishing it with flourishes, details, anecdotes, and mutual ribbing.

3. Use of the pronoun "we" over "I," as in, "That was a great time for us." This is an especially significant indicator of "togetherness" in an LDR. The couple may identify each other's homes as "our home" and each considers him- or herself to have two homes, as opposed to "mine" and "my partner's."

4. An emphasis on overcoming the obstacles, the struggles, the negatives of the relationship.

SIGNS OF AN UNHEALTHY RELATIONSHIP:

1. Remembering any instances from the early period of the relationship as negative. The first bloom of romance should be remembered as a lovely, exciting time, not as "I should've known from the first time I saw his apartment that he was a total slob."

2. A resistance to telling the story, and once prompted, an inclination to keep it short.

3. Use of the pronoun "I" over "we," and a story that sounds more like an account of two separate lives that occasionally bump up against each other rather than the story of a committed couple.

4. An emphasis on the obstacles, the struggles, and the negatives of the relationship, with no stories of triumph to balance them out.

Long-Term Survival: Major Keys to Success

It's certainly useful for you to follow the advice of couples who have been in LDRs and survived. Remember, though, that what worked for them is not necessarily going to work for you. Each relationship is different, and you're going to have to come up with your own ways of making it work.

Maybe you'll decide never to fight over e-mail. Maybe you'll decide to settle arguments exclusively over e-mail. Different modes of communication work differently for each couple. Most important is that you *do* communicate, and that you believe in the relationship enough to withstand all of the lonely in-between times. Here are some of the key pointers

LDPs use to make it through all the trials and tribulations.

Have a set of rules. Decide on a general plan of action regarding how often you'll see each other, how often you'll call/e-mail, and how long you plan to be long distance.

Have an end in sight. It might even help to draw up some sort of "agreement for the future" or "commitment document," just to make sure both of you are thinking along the same lines. If you're not ready to declare an end-date, come up with a deadline for having that first discussion about who's going to relocate.

Develop full lives that are independent of each other. The reality of being in a long-distance relationship is that you will be spending much of your time apart. Instead of waiting until the weekends to live your life, dive into activities and create social situations for yourself between the visits with your partner. Pay attention to your in-town friends and family. Make more friends. Focus on your career. Take classes.

Talk often about the future. Especially when you find yourself getting into little spats about trivial things, take a step back and look at your long-term relationship. Instead of getting caught up in the frustrations that come along with being in an LDR, get some perspective by taking a broader view of your relationship.

Share as many experiences as possible. Relationships are built on shared experiences, which is what makes an LDR fundamentally challenging: Sharing is just logistically difficult when you're hours and sometimes multiple time zones apart. Try to maximize the amount that you share with your partner by using every form of communication possible—text messaging, phone, letters, and so forth. Take vacations together. If one of you has a job that allows you to telecommute for a few days or a week, take your laptop to your partner's home and stay for a week, even if you don't see each other most of the day. There's no substitute for being there to greet her when she gets home from work.

Schedule "relationship talks." The kinds of exchanges that might happen between a couple as they're lying in bed at the end of the day, the taking stock of the relationship to find out what's working and what's not—these discussions are harder to have when you're long distance. Since you don't want to bring up serious relationship topics every time you're lucky enough to be together, schedule a time when you can bring everything you've been thinking about to the table, whether it's once a month or once every three months.

Be romantic. L-D partners, especially those who decide to start a relationship based on one night's flirtation and a few phone calls, are likely to be lured by the romance of the scenario. Perhaps they believe in fate, destiny, and love at first sight—their home movie collections are stocked with Meg Ryan movies and Disney offerings.

LDRs provide many opportunities for being especially romantic—from the anticipation you feel about seeing each other again, to the love notes and e-mails you'll surely send to your LDP. Live it up!

Trust each other. It's up for debate whether absence makes the heart grow fonder, but it's a sure thing that absence breeds jealousy in any relationship where the partners do not trust each other completely. Trust is especially hard to forge when you have no way of keeping tabs on the other person. How do you know that she was really at dinner with a friend when you called and not macking on some dude down at the corner bar? Well, if the latter even crosses your mind as a possibility, you need to introduce some honesty into the relationship. Talk about your feelings of mistrust and where they're coming from. And continue to be honest with each other so neither one of you has any reason to make assumptions.

doves	albatrosses
lobsters	wolves
penquin	coyotes
cranes	beavers
pigeons	gibbons
parrots	dik-diks
geese	prairie voles
swans	whales

Who's Going to Relocate?

"Relocation wasn't a question for me. She had a more compelling reason to be where she was [in law school]. I felt like most of our energy was spent getting to each other on the weekends; it took five hours each way."
—Neil

When put in practical terms, relocation should be a relatively easy decision. Who has the higher-paying job? Who has the more portable job (e.g., freelancing, teaching)? Some people are involved in very specialized careers and can study or work in only a few places. Others, including academics, are in such highly competitive careers that they are forced to move in order to have a job at all. If one LDP is in an inflexible situation, the other has to be prepared to relocate.

So many logistics! LDR could just as easily be an acronym for Logistics-Dominated Relationship. This relocation issue could be the final logistical decision that you make as an LDR couple. Just one observation before you take the leap: some experts advise getting a commitment in writing or in the form of an engagement ring before any long-distance moves are made. (These experts include some relationship therapists and most meddling mothers.) That's up to you. Just be sure you're in agreement over where you stand and what, exactly, comprises the game plan.

Both LDPs should fill out the following questionnaire, ascribing "true" or "false" to each statement:

1. **My job is not portable—I can't do it from anywhere, and it would be difficult for me to find a job doing something similar in another location.**
   ☐ True
   ☐ False

2. **I'm in school or the military.**
   ☐ True
   ☐ False

3. **I have human dependents who live either with me or nearby.**
   ☐ True
   ☐ False

4. I own (as opposed to rent) my house/apartment.
   ☐ True
   ☐ False

5. I live near my family (and am close with them).
   ☐ True
   ☐ False

6. I make more money than my LDP.
   ☐ True
   ☐ False

7. I suffer from neophobia (fear of new things and new experiences).
   ☐ True
   ☐ False

Tally your results. The LDP with the most "true"s will have more difficulty relocating.

Negotiation Tactics

"Relocation frustration" is a condition characterized by a lack of clarity about the question: Who should move? Sometimes a simple quiz like the preceding one is not enough to decide this important matter. It's typical for both partners to be reluctant to pack up their lives, bid good-bye to their friends, quit their jobs, and make the ultimate sacrifice for the other person, even if they're confident their LDP is the love of their life. This is where negotiation tactics come in.

Negotiation is all about getting other people to do what they wouldn't intuitively decide to do, or to change their mind about a decision they've already made. When it comes to LDR relocation, be aware of the subtle mind games that may come into play, both from your end as well as your partner's. Here are some strategies for getting past no, adapted from the worlds of business and politics.

STRATEGY #1: KNOW YOUR AND YOUR LDP'S HOT BUTTONS
This allows you to press hers during negotiation and to protect yours from being pressed. Maybe one of the traits she loves about you is how close you are to your family—use that to demonstrate why you need to stay put: "I don't want to move so far from my sister and my parents. Mom and Dad are getting older. I want to spend time with them before

they're gone."

If one of your hot buttons is a fear of appearing selfish, beware of your LDP trying to milk this fear for his own gain. "Why is everything always about you?" he might say. Instead of having a knee-jerk emotional reaction, stop and think: *Is* it always about you? Have past negotiations ended in your favor? Probably not exclusively.

STRATEGY #2: BUY TIME

Especially if an ultimatum has been issued, or if emotions are running high, take a moment to stop, take a deep breath, maybe inject some humor into the conversation. Suggest that the two of you sleep on it or think about it for a few days before taking up the subject again.

STRATEGY #3: USE "SALAMI TACTICS" OR THE TACTICS OF EROSION

In the early 1950s, the leader of the Communist party in Hungary, Matyas Rakosi, adopted a strategy known as "salami tactics" to consolidate power. He used a gradual progression of threats and alliances as a means of overcoming opposition. Take a page from his book and focus on making alliances of your own. Get your mutual friends on *your* side, especially the ones who have influence over your LDP.

STRATEGY #4: KEEP IT NICE

Agree whenever you can—listen and paraphrase your partner's thoughts to show you're listening. Acknowledge his
points. Don't provoke: Use "and" rather than "but" when
you're responding to your LDP's points. Ask for his advice—
what would he do if he were in your shoes? This will both
flatter him and make him more empathetic.

Preparing to Move

Once one of you has decided to make the move, you'll need
to say good-bye to your old life and build a new one in your
new town. It's not enough that your partner is going to be
there. You'll need to create a life apart from him or her, too.
Here are some guidelines for doing just that:

**Before you move, start looking for a new job in your new
location.** Career counselor Andrea Kay advises that you start
by consulting your hometown network. Set up meetings with
people at home. "Sit down with them and have a meaningful conversation about your goals," Kay says. "Get their
advice. Ask them, 'Do you know any people there I can contact to get to know the market better?'" Note the subtlety
here—you're not out and out asking them to find you a job.

Before you move, Kay says, make an extended visit—one

or two weeks—and meet with the people you've contacted in your hometown. Again, don't ask them to find you a job—the meetings should be purely informational. At the end of the meeting, leave a résumé with them in case they hear of anything opening up. "The best way to get in the door anywhere is to get referred," says Kay.

Start setting up a support system. Research clubs you can join, organizations where you can volunteer. Again, consult people at home and ask everyone if they know people you can contact in your new location.

Go out with a bang. Throw yourself a good-bye party. Invite everyone in your life and let them tell you how much they're going to miss you. Include your new address and contact information on the party invite.

 Megan A. and Ben were in an SLDR. They met through a mutual friend when Megan was in San Francisco for a work-related conference. The two exchanged e-mail addresses, and when Megan returned to New York, they e-mailed constantly. Soon they exchanged phone numbers and planned another visit. Six months later, Megan moved to San Francisco—and moved in with Ben. "It was so out of character for me to just pick up and move, but I was ready to leave New York, and visiting him, I had fallen in love with San Francisco," says Megan. "It was just the right place, the right person, and the right time."

COUPLE CASE STUDY

Megan A., 28, healthcare exec, and Ben, 31, computer programmer

Dependents/pets: 0

Distance: New York City to San Francisco = 2,906 miles

L-D for: Six months

Frequency of visits: Five visits in all; two were week-long

Their advice: Prepare to be terrified when you relocate. "I cried the whole five hours on the plane," says Megan, who made the move to the West Coast. "That doesn't mean you're doing the wrong thing. If you decide to live together as soon as you relocate, know that if the living situation doesn't work out, that may just mean you rushed into living together too soon, not that you should break up."

Status at press time: Married

To Live Together or Not

Dr. Neil Clark Warren, author of *Finding the Love of Your Life*, advises LDPs who have lived away from each other for at least a year and a half to spend six months living in the same city, either apart or together, before taking the marriage leap. (He and his wife, Marylyn, followed that guideline and have a successful 40-year marriage to show for it.)

The same clear-eyed decision-making is called for when it comes to LDPs moving in together. Unless you've lived together before, you may want to move more gradually into each other's lives: The LDP relocating to his partner's home should consider looking for his own place. Should you play it safe and move into your own place, here are some ways to know when it's time to take the next step:

You know it's time for you to start living together when . . .

- You're spending more than four nights a week at your LDP's place.

- You've forgotten what your own apartment looks like.

- Your LDP asks you to start chipping in on utility bills.

- Your voice is on your LDP's answering machine.

- You've become accustomed to your LDP's hair on your bathroom floor.

- You've discussed how you'll handle finances.

- You've talked about and agreed on your commitment level, and if you're headed for marriage, set a time limit on how long you'll live together before you get engaged.

The good news about moving in: Relationship experts advise couples to wait to move in together until their relationship has been tested by conflict. You and your partner have already overcome one huge relationship hurdle—distance. This bodes well for your success.

Congratulations! You are now living a close-range relationship.

Surviving the Long-Distance Breakup

Chances are that distance will be the catalyst rather than the cause of your long-distance breakup. Would you have broken up anyway? It's quite likely. Often, the distance will reveal early on that you're not meant to be: LDRs require more of an early commitment than regular close-range relationships, and both partners have to devote equal parts time (talking on the telephone, traveling to meet the other person), money (phone bills, travel expenses, pet sitters, more dinners out), and sacrifice.

LDRs are on the path of greatest resistance—and in order for them to work, both partners have to be fully invested in the relationship. If one of you is not, this will become evident more quickly than it would in a close-range relationship.

After you've analyzed your relationship and determined that it won't, in fact, go the distance, it's time to bring it to a close. Long-distance relationships provide possibly the only exception to the rule "Never break it off over the phone." Oftentimes it's simply not feasible to fly across the country to have "the talk" and then turn around and fly home. Of course, if your LDP is just a few hours away by car or train, you should break it off in person. (Don't drop the bomb at the end of a weekend visit, though.) Breakups are never easy, and you should be prepared for the requisite mourning period after you and your partner say your final good-byes. You'll be sad, but wiser. (And on the up side, you'll have gained a ton of frequent flyer miles. Go ahead and take a long vacation.)

Pros

■ The Golden Rule—"Always break up face to face, never over the phone"—is waived when you have to travel three hours by plane to get to that person.

■ Your phone bill and commuting expenses will decrease, leaving you with plenty of funds to do the requisite post-breakup boozing and excessive shopping.

■ You'll have much more time on the weekends to spend with friends in your own town. (And if you moved to a new place, you'll actually get to enjoy it at your leisure, every weekend.)

■ It's easier to get over someone when you're used to not having him around.

■ There's very little chance of an awkward post-breakup encounter.

■ You're free to buy clothes that wrinkle easily.

Cons

- Getting dumped over the phone is humiliating and horrible no matter how far away the other person is.

- Your acquisition of frequent flyer miles will come to a stand-still.

- You won't have any friends in your hometown to distract you, because you spent most of your weekends with the person who has suddenly dropped out of your life.

- It will be harder to find out what your ex is up to, whether she's dating anyone else, and if she's completely distraught over the fact that she stupidly broke up with you.

- There's less of a chance of him running into you with your fabulous new boyfriend.

- You're left with a lifetime supply of travel-sized cosmetics and toiletries.

It's all too easy to avoid confrontation and dodge your partner's emails and phone calls until he gets the message that it's over. But you must face your demons and do your duty. If it's too hard to say that you've simply lost interest or that you can no longer be with someone who writes such incredibly boring e-mails, try the old standby: "It's not you. It's not me. It's the distance."

Living Happily Ever After

Did your LDR survive? Congratulations. You're a graduate of LDR University, whose student body is growing every year. Now stop congratulating yourself and use your wisdom and experience to school others who are in LDRs. They need your help. Shower them with hope. And keep working on your own relationship.

Though chances are your LDR is much stronger now than it was when it first began, there will still be storms to weather. Consult this book now and again: Retake the VAT on page 92 when you're feeling dissatisfied about your time together. And if you weren't fully ready to face "Chapter 6: The Future" at this point in your LDR, earmark it for now and come back to it when you're prepared to take the next step.

If your LDR did not survive, don't be surprised if you're among the many LDR alumni who swear never *ever* to get into another LDR. And don't be surprised, either, if eventually you find yourself in, yes, yet another long-distance relationship.

Here you are, a long-distance love expert, accustomed to exercising all of the skills you've learned and honed over the months and years apart. The good news: Many of these skills are still relevant. For example, making communication a priority will serve you well even after one of you has moved and you're living together in the same town. Many people in close-distance relationships (CDRs, or those that occur when two people are living in the same geographic region) sometimes feel as if they're long-distance, even when they're living in the same house. And you may feel this way, too, someday. If so, your LDR skills will come in handy.

But when you first jump into this new phase of your relationship—when you go from long-distance to close-distance—there are some major adjustments to make. You'll need to work some different muscles to make the transition into a fully functional (or a garden-variety dysfunctional) close-distance duo.

How to Adapt Once You're in the Same Place

Everything's been building up to this. Whether you started long-distance or turned long-distance, your eyes have never left the prize: the day you would finally live in the same zip code. And that day has arrived—yippee! Congratulations and please take a moment to bask in your couple-y glow.

Okay, now, are you ready? Because it's not that easy. No matter whether you've decided to move in together or to maintain separate addresses, you may be having some second thoughts after the initial excitement has faded. You may be asking yourself:

■ **Has she always been so consistently late for every date/so untidy/such a rowdy drunk?**

It doesn't really matter which descriptor you choose for the end of this sentence. The point is: Every little quirk that you once encountered intensely and for relatively short periods of time is magnified tenfold once you're living in the same place.

You may feel an initial wave of panic, as in, "Have I made a mistake here?," and "Do I really know this person?" Close your eyes, envision something peaceful, and let the wave wash over you. It's completely normal to feel this way. You *do* know this person, but you've only gotten to know him in short bursts, and it's likely he was on better behavior during your visits than he is day-to-day.

This is the same panic newlyweds felt in olden days when no one lived together (or really even got to know each other) before they married. After the excitement of the wedding night dissipated, the panic set in, and the new bride and

To help you through the muddle, here's a list of things that close-distance couples should and shouldn't do on a regular basis:

Dos

- Do check with each other before making weeknight plans.

- Do eat dinner together, but just as often don't.

- Do talk in person as opposed to on the phone or via texting.

- Do sleep over regularly.

- Do fight over the remote control.

- Do get sick of each other.

- Do take the $278 you used to spend every month on travel, telephone bills and other L-D expenses and store it in a Fabulous Vacation Fund.

Don'ts

- Don't spend every second of free time together.

- Don't recount the details of your breakfast and/or other seemingly trivial facts about your day when you talk. (When you're living it, you don't need the rundown.)

- Don't end each phone conversation with "I miss you terribly. I can't wait until I see you again."

- Don't stash pieces of your clothing under your LDP's pillow so he or she can remember your smell.

- Don't buy travel-sized toiletries.

- Don't complain to your friends about not having a date to the office holiday party.

- Don't consistently arrive late to work claiming your train/plane was delayed or because of traffic.

groom pondered endless vistas of misery—will I be picking his dirty socks up off the floor every day for the rest of my life? Will I be eating meatloaf that's gritty as sand every Thursday night for the rest of my life?

Yes, the answer is you *will* be picking up his dirty socks and eating her nasty meatloaf, but this is the price you pay to be in close proximity to all of those wonderful qualities that drew you to her in the first place. Try to remember those qualities, and remind yourself of them frequently as you navigate your way through this initial adjustment period.

■ **Why are all of my friends and family so ecstatically happy?**
They are happy because your dicey and unstable (solely in their eyes) situation seems to be resolved at last.

■ **I should be ecstatically happy. What's wrong with me?**
See first question, page 197.

■ **But really, don't give me that "see page 197" crap. Why does this feel so weird?!**
You are essentially a new couple in an established couple's clothing. Yes, you've been dating for many months or even many years. Yes, your relationship has withstood major challenges, and you've invested massive amounts of time,

money, and emotional equity in this relationship. At the same time, you've been living a totally compartmentalized life—single on the weekdays, in a relationship on the weekends. You have no idea how to relate to each other on a day-to-day basis. The weirdness comes from figuring this out. You thought the hard part was over. It's not.

■ **How long does the adjustment period last?**
I'd give it a good three months.

Majoring in LDRs

Long-distance relationships have become a common enough phenomenon to merit study by researchers and scholars—there are more than 100 papers published on the different aspects of meeting, relating, communicating, maintaining, and thriving (or not). This is a happy development, as LDRs are a very rich area for potential research. Note that the majority of studies looking at LDRs focus mainly on those in which the partners have at one time lived in the same place. Attention psych majors: This area of research is just waiting to be tackled.

Many of the conclusions drawn in the LDR studies are consistent with those drawn from simple anecdotal observations. For your edification, a few scholarly tidbits:

- Those who have already experienced relationships in which little time is spent with a partner are more likely to thrive in a long-distance relationship.

- Those who maintain the perspective that there's a constructive reason for the separation—for example, that the schooling or job that led to the separation is for the betterment of both partners' futures—are more likely to be satisfied.

- Those who have a strong commitment to their professional lives are more likely to thrive in an LDR.

- Those who are in LDRs are less afraid of intimacy than those who are in close-distance relationships.

- The single most common factor to which successful LDPs attribute their success is maintaining good communication.

- LDPs are more likely than those in CDRs to focus on future plans as a means of keeping their relationship vital.

- Frequency of visits is not a good predictor of relationship satisfaction.

Part of the experience of writing a book on LDRs is having the chance to hear other LDPs' tales of heartbreak and triumph. Along the way there've been some awe-inspiring romantic sentiments broached from afar. This hall of fame pays tribute to those LDPs who:

■ Shipped a gallon of homemade chicken-noodle soup (complete with a heart-shaped carrot) and a pair of his ski socks to his LDP while she was miserable with a bad cold.

■ Swept his LDP off to the honeymoon suite at a swank hotel during her first visit, so she could experience the town in style.

■ Sent her LDP off on a six-week business trip over the holidays with a bag of gifts and instructions not to open them until Christmas, New Year's, his birthday, and some randomly selected days, just because.

■ Called a Chinese restaurant in his LDP's neighborhood and had her favorite dishes delivered while she was freaking out about finishing a huge paper due the next day.

■ Sent his LDP a homemade film panning over the places that meant a lot to them in their former shared hometown, set to a soundtrack of sappy songs and "their songs."

■ On the other hand, people in long-distance relationships who had some face-to-face contact within a six-month period were more satisfied than those who had none.

■ Those in nonmonogamous LDRs are less likely to be satisfied with the relationship.

■ Those who have a positive role model—for example, a friend or family member who has married a former LDP—are more likely to be satisfied and optimistic about their own situation.

■ The frustration caused by not being around to give someone a hug can lead to stupid arguments about trivial things.

■ The best way to stop feeling lonely is to stop dwelling on the fact that you're missing your partner by refocusing your energies on schoolwork or professional work, or by leaning on your network of friends.

Questions and Answers

When *The Long-Distance Relationship Guide* first came out, I began to receive lots of requests for advice. Many were repeats of the same types of questions. Here's a sampling, along with my answers:

Discussing Exclusivity

Q: I'm a New Yorker who "e-met" someone from Phoenix a month ago. We hit it off, and we continue to e-mail and talk to each other on the phone daily. However, we have yet to meet in person. I continue to get new e-mails from other potential dates, and I don't know exactly how to answer them. I don't really want to send them away in case this acquaintance from Phoenix does not work out. I've also noticed that he is online a fair amount of time.

I'm okay with this, but it got me to thinking, what are the signs that someone might continue to be looking and possibly leading you on? He seems like he might be the person worth fighting for, although it would be good to know where he sat so I could be either relieved or move on. Where in the dating process do you make that decision on exclusivity?

A: I would think that you'd both want to keep your options open until you meet in person. At the same time, it wouldn't hurt to bring "cyber-exclusivity" up with him, either over e-mail or on the phone, in a nonthreatening way, to see if he's been thinking about this, too. I'm sure it's been on his mind as well, and it would be reassuring for both of you to know that you share similar concerns. (And if he doesn't share these concerns, that might be equally illuminating.)

Number One Piece of Advice

Q: What is your number one piece of advice for people who are in long-distance relationships?

A: Stay optimistic. Lots of people will tell you that LDRs never work out, but studies instead indicate that the success rate of LDRs is actually equivalent to that of short-distance relationships.

Taking the Pulse of the Relationship

Q: I live in Mexico, and I met a man when he was here on vacation. We spent 14 days together, and then he went back home to New York. Those 14 days were really a strong thing— we got really attached, and the goodbye was very sad. After that we e-mailed a lot, almost every day. Then he came back to see me, and now we write every day and we have phone calls every 15 days, more or less.

He's going to continue to keep trying to come to see me, and I will try to see him, but it's very expensive. I don't know what will happen. I don't want to rush, but I want to keep this thing going. I'm very happy with this guy. . . . I want to enjoy it and not create expectations, but it is impossible not to think about the future sometimes. We obviously have not talked about any future yet! What is your advice for us?

A: It sounds like the two of you are putting a lot of time and effort into making this work, which is great. Too often someone will write to me and describe a situation where one person is doing most of the heavy lifting. But if both of you are equally committed to the relationship, that's an excellent sign.

I do think that you answered your own question. In order to progress to the next step, you need to have a serious talk about the future. Long-distance relationships force you into having these talks sooner than you would have if you were in the same place, so it might feel weird, but at this point, you need to know certain things (such as, Can either of you see yourself moving? Are you both in this for the long haul?) in order to justify continuing to invest so much money, emotion, and time.

Q: My partner and I are separated by two coasts and have been together for almost three years. Within the first year, he made plans to move to California, where we could be together. After trying to make arrangements with his employer and family, he decided after six months that he could not make the move. This was a year and a half ago. My main problem is that he does not want to change his living arrangements now or in the foreseeable future; in other words, he is content with the status quo. I, on the other hand, would like some commitment that this relationship will go to the next level. He continues to ask me to be patient without assurance. Do you have any advice for us?

A: I hear about situations like this a lot, which is why I suggest that people talk sooner rather than later to forecast an endpoint. I completely understand why you're frustrated, especially since you've been dating for three years.

I think you need to have a serious talk with him about the future. No more waiting around—you need to know the answers to certain questions about moving and marriage to justify continuing to invest so much emotion and time in the relationship. He can ask you to wait without assurance only for so long. Instead of putting him on the spot immediately, let him know that you need answers to these questions and then set a date with him in the near future to have this talk.

Be clear with him about your needs, then reassess the situation after hearing him out.

Using the Distance as an Excuse for Breaking Up

Q: Did you ever find in your research that "it's the distance" as a reason for ending an LDR can sometimes be used to hide other "issues" someone may have?

A: I have certainly heard of people attributing the demise of their LDR to the distance. Whether they were using this as an excuse to mask other issues, I just don't know. The distance is definitely a handy excuse for a person who's looking for an easy way out, but it's also true that some people aren't cut out for LDRs. They simply may get into one only to discover that they crave the day-to-day physical presence of a partner.

Am I Crazy?

Q: I met someone online, and we e-mail and talk on the phone all the time. We have everything in common except the 1,500 miles between us. We're hoping to actually meet in person soon. I'm wondering what your thoughts are on this situation. Is it crazy to hope that this might work out? Some of my friends seem to think so, and so do some of his.

I feel like the most important thing right now is to be honest with each other—we both have agreed that if we walked away from this right now, we would always wonder what could have happened. I'm usually someone who has a clear picture of what's going on in life and what's going to happen—but I'm at a loss now. Is there something we could be doing differently?

A: When I was writing my book, I discovered that a lot of people meet online, get to know each other over the phone and over e-mail, then eventually meet and fall in love and end up living happily ever after. I also found that a lot of people meet online, get to know each other over the phone and over e-mail, and eventually meet in person and realize there's no connection. So, to summarize, basically, yes, it may work out and yes, it may not work out, and I think you're right to give it a chance by meeting in person. I don't think you can know for sure if there's chemistry until you're face-to-face.

Your friends are worried about your getting your hopes up and about your investing a lot of time, emotion, and energy in an uncertain situation. The fact that they're worried means they are good friends—you're lucky to have them. You should hear their concerns, try to remain grounded in reality, and understand the dangers of getting to know each other from a distance. (There's a dangerous tendency to idealize the other person, remember.)

As far as whether it will work out with 1,500 miles between you, this is something to worry about after you meet. Many LDRs do work out in the end, but both partners need to be fully committed (it's a lot of hard work and a lot of frustration), and ultimately one of you needs to be willing to move.

Most importantly, *please* make sure that you meet in a public place. You might feel like you know him well, but it's always best to be safe.

Appendix A
LDR Survival from A to Z

Your LDR will be much easier to navigate once you and your partner add these items to your lexicon.

Aural sex: Otherwise known as phone sex.

Blackberry: To receive your partner's e-mails when you're away from your computer on a hand-held device. Also, a **box** to store your love letters.

Car: Especially if your partner is within driving distance, and if not, to get you to and from the airport. Also, **clothes** that travel well.

Digital camera: To take pictures of yourself after you've colored your hair orange, of your garden the first day it blooms tulips, of the soufflé you made that came out perfectly—to e-mail to your LDP.

Everyday contact: By e-mail, phone, text messaging, or telegram.

Frequent flyer miles: Use a credit card that lets you accrue them with each purchase. Pay your phone bill with this credit card. Also, supportive **friends** and **family**.

Garment bag: For transporting the suit you'll put on before you commute back for work on Monday morning. Also, a **gas card**.

Humor: To make it through the lonely stretches and through bad travel days when everything goes wrong—gridlock traffic, canceled flight, caught in hail storm, etc.

Independence: If you don't have any, get some. You're going to need to create a life for yourself that keeps you fulfilled and busy.

Journal: To write down your feelings.

Kava kava: To ease your nerves while you're traveling. (There's also St. John's wort or the old standby, Valium.)

Luggage: For traveling—it should be small enough to fit into an overhead compartment and preferably be on wheels.

Monogamy: Seeing other people never works.

Notes: And letters that remind your LDP about how you feel. Leave notes behind for your partner if you are visiting. If you are the one being visited, place a note in her luggage for her to find when she returns home.

Open mind: To accept all of the unexpected situations that may arise during the course of the LDR.

Psychotherapy: It never hurts. Also, **postage, postcards**, and a **pet sitter**.

Quicken: Or some other computer program to help you keep track of your finances, so you can figure your new phone and travel expenses into your budget.

Romance: To keep the spark alive, even when you're far apart. Send flowers for no reason, or a love letter.

Surprise visits: A necessary form of romance. So are hand-written letters on **stationery**. Also, a strong **support system** at home.

Telephone: If you're not a phone person, become one. Also, procure a **train schedule**, **travel-size cosmetics** and **toiletries**, and **trust**.

Understanding: Because you are going to have to make and accept more compromises than if you were a close-range couple.

Videophone: Get one that you can hook up to your cell phone or your computer.

Willingness to travel: Because you'll be traveling a lot.

Xanax: To treat your anxiety disorder after X months of being apart.

Yoga: Or some other physical exercise to keep your body and mind occupied during the times when you're not together.

Zeal: And a deep commitment to your relationship.

Appendix B
A Concise Glossary of L-D Terms

Close-distance relationship (CDR): One that occurs while two people are living in the same geographic region.

Commuter marriage: An LDR between married partners.

Expiration dating: A fling defined by the mutual understanding that nothing long-term will come of this series of encounters, whether it lasts for a weekend or two weeks. This is often the case when two people are visiting the same place for vacation or on business.

Long-distance courtship: When two people attempt to begin a long-term relationship from a distance, getting to know each other via phone conversations, e-mails, and letter writing. Often grows out of aborted expiration dating and has expectations of turning into a relationship.

Middle-distance relationship: When partners are between one and three hours' driving time apart.

Stand-in boyfriend/girlfriend: The platonic friend ultimately made by either the leaver or leavee to replace the constant companionship of the absent partner. The stand-in fills in at parties, movies, and other social occasions, and often mysteriously disappears during weekends when the partner is visiting. (Dangerous territory is entered when the stand-in's name is dropped once every three sentences during phone conversations.)

Relocation frustration: The feeling that results when a long-distance relationship comes to a turning point and partners must decide that one must move to join the other in order to make the relationship work. The frustration derives from the constant negotiation and compromises that are made in deciding who's going to move. (Note: This term can also describe the period directly after the move, when the two partners are adjusting to their new living situation.)

ACKNOWLEDGMENTS

The irony of this book is that it got the green light the day after LDP #1 and I parted ways. So thanks are due to Mindy Brown, my editor, for showing me the humor within that predicament and for teasing the bitterness out of the first draft. Thanks are also due to LDP #1 for coming up with the idea for this book. (Too bad you won't see any of the royalties.) Finally, thanks to all of the long-distance partners who let me ask them extremely personal questions and to the military wives and truckers' wives who contributed such creative and useful advice. If I had the time, I would make each and every one of you a mixed tape.